Becoming a Growth Mindset School

Becoming a Growth Mindset School explores the theories which underpin a growth mindset ethos and lays out how to embed them into the culture of a school. It offers step-by-step guidance for school leaders to help build an approach to teaching and learning that will encourage children to embrace challenge, persist in the face of setback, and see effort as the path to mastery. The book isn't about quick fixes or miracle cures, but an evidence-based transformation of the way we think and talk about teaching, leading, and learning.

Drawing upon his own extensive experience and underpinned by the groundbreaking scholarship of Carol Dweck, Angela Duckworth, and others, Chris Hildrew navigates the difficulties, practicalities, and opportunities presented by implementing a growth mindset, such as:

- forming a growth mindset curriculum

- launching a growth mindset with staff

- marking, assessing, and giving feedback with a growth mindset

- growth mindset misconceptions and potential mistakes

- family involvement with a growth mindset.

Innovatively and accessibly written, this thoroughly researched guide shows how a growth mindset ethos benefits the whole school community, from its students and teachers to parents and governors. *Becoming A Growth Mindset School* will be of invaluable use to all educational leaders and practitioners.

Chris Hildrew is Headteacher at Churchill Academy & Sixth Form, UK. He has launched and developed a growth mindset ethos as Deputy Headteacher at Chew Valley School and as Headteacher at Churchill Academy & Sixth Form. Chris also provides training to other schools wishing to embed a growth mindset ethos.

Becoming a Growth Mindset School

The Power of Mindset to Transform Teaching, Leadership and Learning

Chris Hildrew

Routledge
Taylor & Francis Group

LONDON AND NEW YORK

First published 2018
by Routledge
2 Park Square, Milton Park, Abingdon, Oxon OX14 4RN

and by Routledge
711 Third Avenue, New York, NY 10017

Routledge is an imprint of the Taylor & Francis Group, an informa business

British Library Cataloguing-in-Publication Data
A catalogue record for this book is available from the British Library

Library of Congress Cataloging-in-Publication Data
Names: Hildrew, Chris, author.
Title: Becoming a growth mindset school : the power of mindset to transform
    teaching, learning and learners / Chris Hildrew.
Description: Abingdon, Oxon ; New York, NY : Routledge, 2018. | Includes
    bibliographical references and index.
Identifiers: LCCN 2017045927 (print) | LCCN 2017059363 (ebook) |
    ISBN 9781315179506 (ebook) | ISBN 9781138895492 (hbk) |
    ISBN 9781138895508 (pbk) | ISBN 9781315179506 (ebk)
Subjects: LCSH: Academic achievement—Psychological aspects. | School
    environment—Psychological aspects. | Motivation in education.
Classification: LCC LB1062.6 (ebook) | LCC LB1062.6 .H54 2018 (print) |
    DDC 370.15/2—dc23
LC record available at https://lccn.loc.gov/2017045927

ISBN: 978-1-138-89549-2 (hbk)
ISBN: 978-1-138-89550-8 (pbk)
ISBN: 978-1-315-17950-6 (ebk)

Typeset in Melior
by Apex CoVantage, LLC

For Dad and Grandad, Hildrew headteachers before me: I hope I make you proud.

For Sam, Emily, and Joseph: I couldn't be prouder of you.

For Janine: with love.

Contents

Foreword

Too often in our culture, new ideas on learning emerge to gain brief fashionable traction, then get turned upon by members of the educational Twitterati and end up being sidelined or debunked or lost or abandoned.

That's why I like Chris Hildrew's book so much.

The truth is that it isn't just a book about growth mindset. It's deeper and richer than that. It's about how as leaders we can lead learning, helping every child from every background to achieve their best – and simultaneously doing the same for the staff in our schools and colleges.

It is a book that is rooted in the optimism of educational opportunity. Using the research of Carol Dweck and others as its starting point, it's an exploration of what happens when we stop labelling and categorising student and teacher and, instead, do what is needed to unleash their potential.

It's most definitely not a book of cheap gimmicks or tick lists. It's about methodology, how we can translate a philosophy based on understanding human effort and convert it into success. Thus, in the course of these pages, we read about character development, engaging parents and families, and insights into staff development.

This, in other words, is a book that takes us to the heart of what education should be – an understanding of the human dynamic in learning. There's a recognition that systems, of course, matter. Rigour matters. Monitoring and routines and management all matter. But they shouldn't be our drivers for improvement.

Thus we get a book with a refreshingly personal voice, a huge range of examples, and an underpinning rationale that demonstrates time and again that we ignore human potential at our peril. There's nothing soppy or anodyne in this. Chris Hildrew demonstrates how such an approach can be transformational to a school's culture – and to the achievements of students and staff.

Becoming a Growth Mindset School is one of those books that takes us back to first principles about how we learn, how we teach, and how we maximise the power to do both better. It's an enlightening read, a sometimes reassuring, sometimes challenging thesis. I gained a lot from it, and I am sure you will too.

Geoff Barton, September 2017

Acknowledgements

This book owes much to the researchers who have dedicated themselves to trying to figure out what works in schools and education. Thank you for building the foundations and for helping us to ask more intelligent questions.

My own teaching and leadership style is a patchwork quilt stitched together from other people's ideas and examples. If I have ever worked with you in a school, you will have had an influence on me. Thank you.

The online teaching and leadership community has changed my thinking beyond measure. Thank you to all the tweachers in my PLN.

Thank you to all those who have offered their inspiration, example, and wisdom in formulating a growth mindset ethos, in particular John Tomsett, James Kerfoot, Shaun Allison, Vic Goddard, Ashley Loynton, Rebecca Tushingham, and Jo Payne.

Thank you to Mark Mallett and the staff and Governors at Chew Valley School for letting me loose with a bold experiment, and thank you to all the staff and Governors at Churchill Academy & Sixth Form for their trust in me.

Thank you to all the students I have ever taught. You have taught me more about learning than any book I have ever read. In particular Jenni, Chris, Clara and Eleanor, Gemma, Jack and Dean, Poppy, Kellan, Kerri, Becca, Libby and Ben – you have inspired me.

Introduction
Becoming a growth mindset school

Imagine a school where industry and commitment are seen as virtues by every member of the community. Where students and staff alike embrace challenges, see effort as the path to mastery, learn from criticism and find lessons and inspiration in the success of others. Where nobody says, "I can't do it" or, worse, "she'll never be able to do it."

Imagine a school where all the staff are united around a common vision. Where every member of staff is engaged in working to develop positive attitudes to learning in the children at the school. Where practice is based in scientific evidence, supported by research and constantly refined in the light of new developments.

Imagine a school where all this is done with compassion and care in a culture which values honesty about failures and mistakes, seeing them not as labels but as opportunities to learn.

This is what it would look like, sound like and feel like to work in a growth mindset school.

And this is the kind of school I want to lead.

As a Deputy Head, my school was successful. The students were proud of their school. They behaved well. But I knew that they could achieve more – that they should be doing better than they were. Staff were working incredibly hard, engaged in a seemingly never-ending round of catch-up and extra-curricular revision sessions. Every year we kept saying, "we have to get it right in Key Stage 3 so that we don't have to do all this last-minute intervention with Year 11." But every year the data showed that Year 11 needed intervention – and fast! – if we were to get the results that were needed to keep Ofsted away. And that the students deserved, of course. We mustn't forget that. So we ploughed our time, resources and energy into Year 11 again, determined that next year we would get it right in Key Stage 3. Next year.

Next year finally came for me when I first came across the idea of growth mindset. I discovered the research of Carol Dweck and others in a TEDx talk by Eduardo Briceño. In his talk, Briceño outlined how Dweck's research shows that people hold different beliefs about their intelligence and ability. Those in what

Dweck calls a "fixed mindset" believe that their intelligence and ability is fixed, immutable, and impossible to change. Opposed to this, others believe that their intelligence and ability could change and improve. Over the course of ten minutes, ideas and thoughts that I had always half realised came into sharper focus and arrayed themselves around the core of Briceño's argument. He concluded:

> how is it possible that, as a society, we are not asking schools to develop a growth mindset in children? Our myopic effort to teach them facts, concepts and even critical thinking skills is likely to fail if we don't also deliberately teach them the essential beliefs that will allow them to succeed not only in school but also beyond.[1]

It seemed to make so much sense. That it was students' own beliefs about their own ability that impacted on their success. That by helping students to understand that their abilities could change and develop – not just by telling them, but by showing them – the growth mindset could be developed. It was, of course, what every good teacher had always tried to do – instil a belief that everyone can succeed. But here it was, codified, researched, evidenced, proven. I needed to find out more!

So began my growth mindset journey. I read Dweck's seminal and accessible work, *Mindset*,[2] over one weekend and started to think about how the ideas could be applied to my own school. There were models already out there, and I eagerly signed up to present a session at a free conference (the Teaching and Learning Takeover 2013, or #TLT13) in Southampton on a Saturday just so I could hear John Tomsett speak about how he had begun to "systematically transform [his] school so that a Growth Mindset attitude runs through it likes [sic] the words in a stick of seaside rock."[3] By the end of #TLT13 in Southampton, I was convinced that this was the work that I had ahead of me. I needed to transform my own school so that every member of the school community saw industry and commitment as virtues and every person understood the principles of mindsets and recognised that, as Dweck herself says, "no matter what your ability is, effort is what ignites that ability and turns it into accomplishment."[4]

After almost a year of planning, we launched our growth mindset ethos the following September. My experience of leading the change has taught me much about implementing whole-school strategy, leadership, and what growth mindset is (and what it isn't), as well as a great deal about myself. We continued to develop and refine our approach as we went, learning from experience what worked and what didn't. Throughout it all, my belief that getting mindsets right is at the core of successful school leadership became stronger and stronger. Simply put: it made a difference.

In no small part, it made a difference to me. I applied Dweck's theories to my own practice, developing my own teaching and leadership as I applied for headships. In my applications, I made it clear that the development of a growth mindset ethos was a core element of my vision and values for the school I was going to lead. In my interviews and presentations, I relied on my knowledge of the theory and research and my experience of implementation to provide me with examples of leadership. And now, as Headteacher, I am developing a whole-school growth mindset ethos for a second time.

This book has been born out of those experiences.

In these pages I will explain the theory and research that underpins a growth mindset ethos and how we have gone about implementing those theories in practice across not one, but two schools. Among the things that impress me most about Dweck's theories are that she has not trademarked or copyrighted the term "growth mindset" and she hasn't prescribed a particular methodology or approach. She discovered something interesting and powerful about self-theories and their impact on motivation and success, which she has shared. How to implement those theories successfully on a school- or even system-wide scale is really up to us. This can be as daunting as it is liberating, but I hope this book will help.

Notes

1 Briceño, "The power of belief."
2 Dweck, *Mindset*.
3 Tomsett, "This much I know."
4 Dweck, op. cit., page 41.

Bibliography

Briceño, E. (2012, 18 November). The power of belief: mindset and success. Retrieved 23 December, 2016, from *YouTube*: https://youtu.be/pN34FNbOKXc

Dweck, C. (2012). *Mindset: How You Can Fulfil Your Potential.* London: Robinson.

Tomsett, J. (2013, 20 October). This much I know about . . . developing a Dweck-inspired growth mindset culture. Retrieved 2 June, 2017, from John Tomsett's blog: https://johntomsett.com/2013/10/20/this-much-i-know-about-developing-a-dweck-inspired-growth-mindset-culture/

What is a growth mindset?

Carol Dweck has devoted her life and career to the study of achievement and success. As one of the world's leading researchers in the fields of personality, social, and developmental psychology, she has spent decades exploring beliefs about intelligence and ability, and how those can impact on performance and attainment. Through this raft of studies, she formulated the theory of fixed and growth mindsets, summarised in *Mindset: How You Can Fulfil Your Potential*.[1]

In the fixed mindset, you believe that your qualities are carved in stone. You are born with a certain amount of ability, and that is all there is to it. Some people are better than you. Other people are not as good as you. But your abilities are fixed, and there is nothing you can do about it. Dweck describes how her own experience of education inculcated the fixed mindset, with particular reference to her sixth-grade class:

> Even as a child, I was focused on being smart, but the fixed mindset was really stamped in by Mrs. Wilson, my sixth-grade teacher. . . . She believed that people's IQ scores told the whole story of who they were. We were seated around the room in IQ order, and only the highest-IQ students could be trusted to carry the flag, clap the erasers, or take a note to the principal. Aside from the daily stomachaches she provoked with her judgmental stance, she was creating a mindset in which everyone in the class had one consuming goal—look smart, don't look dumb. Who cared about or enjoyed learning when our whole being was at stake every time she gave us a test or called on us in class?[2]

One of the by-products of the fixed mindset is the impact it has on our own self-image. If we only have a fixed amount of ability, it becomes a priority to demonstrate that we have a lot of it if we are to preserve our self-esteem and status. Therefore, Dweck theorises, in the fixed mindset the priority is to "look smart at all times and at all costs." This leads to the subterfuge of creating an appearance of competence or to the avoidance of situations in which you might be found wanting. I've seen this in the classroom so many times that I have lost count. The students who would rather get sent out than read aloud. Students who become the class clown to avoid having to write at length. Students who hide, shrinking back into themselves as classmates raise their hands, every fibre of their body language reading "please don't pick me, please don't pick me . . ." Why not? Because, if I pick them and they get the answer wrong, they will look stupid. They will look dumb. Their deficiency will be publicised. And this will define them as people – they will be the one that doesn't know the answer.

On the other side of this, however, is the growth mindset. In this mindset, you believe that the abilities and qualities you are born with can be developed and cultivated through effort, application, experience, and practice. With the growth mindset in place, we see challenging situations as opportunities to learn and grow. When we make a mistake in our reading or writing, we learn from it and improve the next time we come across that word or that expression. When the teacher asks a question, we think about it, and we are happy to explore it together with our classmates to help refine and develop our thinking, leading to greater and deeper understanding. The process helps us to improve. To grow. And even if we don't know the answer right now, if we work at it, listen carefully and apply ourselves, we will know it soon. In the growth mindset, Dweck suggests, the priority is "learn at all times and at all costs."

These mindsets have implications for our behaviour in learning situations and for the outcomes we are likely to experience. When faced with a challenging task, for example, if we are in a fixed mindset, we are likely to seek to avoid it. What if we fail? That will surely prove that we haven't got what it takes. If we fail, we will *be a failure.* In contrast, in the growth mindset, we will see a challenging task as an opportunity to test ourselves and to learn and grow from the experience. We probably won't get it on the first attempt, but that's not a problem – we will get some of the way there. On our second attempt, we'll get a bit further. On the third, further still. Eventually, we'll crack it. Then we can move on.

The second area where the mindsets have a significant impact on the way we behave is in our attitude to effort. In a fixed mindset, effort should not be needed. If we have the ability, we should be able to do it without trying too hard. If we need to put a lot of effort in, it's a sign that we don't have the ability – and therefore the effort is pointless. In a growth mindset, however, we recognise that effort is necessary in order to grow. As Carl Sagan says, "the brain is like a muscle. When we think well, we feel good. Understanding is a kind of ecstasy."[3]

Third, the mindsets impact the way we respond to criticism. In a fixed mindset, critique of our performance is critique of *us*, of our very being. When we're told we've not done well at something, it is a criticism of our ability and it defines us. However, in a growth mindset, we see critique and feedback as essential to help us grow and improve. We recognise that we won't ever be perfect and that we can continue to improve – not because we aren't good enough, but because we can be even better, to paraphrase Dylan Wiliam.[4]

Finally, our mindset influences the way we see the success of others. In a fixed mindset, we can feel threatened by the success of others because we see them as being *better than us*. This is the mindset that sees the flurry of "what did you get?" questions when an assessment is handed back with a grade on it. What is happening in this situation is that the students are trying to establish their position in the hierarchy of ability in the room. Where do I stand? If I was being taught by Dweck's Mrs Wilson, where would she be sitting me in the room? Towards the top? Or towards the bottom? The learning experience of the feedback from the assessment is invariably lost in the quest to salvage self-esteem. I have seen children rip up their work when they've got it back with a poor grade on it, as though destroying the evidence will prevent it from existing and damaging their self-image. "Look smart at all times and at all costs" taken to extremes.

In a growth mindset, however, we can find lessons and inspiration in the achievement of other people. We want to learn from them. What's their secret? How did they do it? I want to find out so that I can do it too.

As I read *Mindset*, I saw again and again examples pertinent to my own classroom experiences of students exhibiting the fixed mindset and, as a result, limiting their achievement. The frustration of seeing students afraid to try, unwilling to commit to challenging tasks, content to sit back and refusing to push themselves. Here was a wealth of research attributing these behaviours to students' beliefs about their own abilities and, crucially, providing a template to *change* those mindsets.

Growth mindset study I: changing mindsets

One of the studies[5] conducted by Dweck and her colleagues explored how mindsets could be changed. In the study, two groups of students were given study skills workshops. In one workshop, students were presented with a range of study skills and ways of working to help them learn better. In the second workshop, students were given the same study skills, but they were also given an intervention which explained some of the basic neuroscience of learning. They were shown how the brain grows and strengthens when you learn new things.

This was new information to me. I am an English graduate; I don't have any Science qualifications beyond a GCSE. In my teacher training notes, the only reference I could find to cognitive science occurred in one section of my notes (see Figure 1.1). There is just one line there that hints at cognitive science: "[Brain needs] stimuli – forms networks." It strikes me as strange that I got through so much of my career without really understanding what was happening inside the brains of the children I was trying to teach. Perhaps I could have benefitted from Dweck's intervention at an earlier stage. Here is what I have learned about what happens in the brain when we learn something.

Neurons are brain cells; synapses are the connections between neurons. When learning takes place, a new synapse is formed. At first, this connection is fragile and tentative, but every time it is used again it strengthens. Eventually, well-trodden

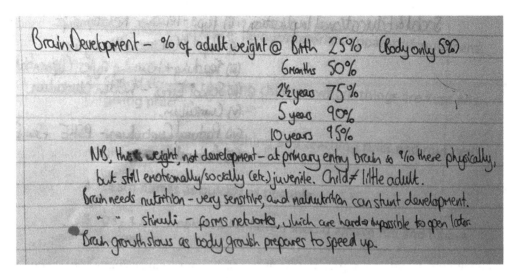

Brain Development – % of adult weight @ Birth 25% (Body only 5%)

6 months 50%

2½ years 75%

5 years 90%

10 years 95%

NB, this is weight, not development – at primary entry brain is 9/10 there physically, but still emotionally/socially (etc.) juvenile. Child ≠ little adult.

Brain needs nutrition – very sensitive, and malnutrition can stunt development.

" " stimuli – forms networks, which are hard → impossible to open later.

Brain growth slows as body growth prepares to speed up.

Figure 1.1 My handwritten PGCE notes, circa 1996

pathways between neurons become networks which can be travelled rapidly, instinctively and unconsciously. This is why I can drive my car without really thinking about it, but why I need to look up the year of Shakespeare's birth every time I want to know it. It's also why our brain can play tricks on us, looking to run through well-established neural networks even when the situation demands a road less travelled.

Neural or synaptic plasticity is the ability of a synaptic connection to develop in strength and efficiency. It is why, if we want students to learn things, we need to get them to repeat them, and why revision – seeing things again – is such an important process. The formation of these neural networks in our brains means that we need to plan for learning which encourages repetition and channels students' energies into building strong, resilient and efficient synaptic connections.

Learning the basics of cognitive science makes sense of the growth mindset. It seems self-evident that the forming of new synaptic connections and the development of strong neural networks is "growth" in the genuine physical sense – the formation of a new or stronger connection in the biology of our brains. The roots of Dweck's "the brain is a muscle – it gets stronger the more you use it" metaphor lie in the growth of the brain's synaptic connections.

Students in Dweck's study were provided with an overview of cognitive science and neural plasticity alongside the study skills which formed the content of the workshop for the control group of students. Teachers didn't know which workshop students were attending, but they reported seeing significant impacts on the motivation and achievement of those who had attended the growth mindset workshop. And it didn't stop there: those in the growth mindset workshop showed an improvement in their grades in mathematics, leading to them outperforming those students in the control group, who had been given the study skills alone.

Implications for practice

It seems so simple: explain how the brain works, then sit back and watch whilst student achievement rockets upwards. Of course, it's never that simple! But essentially, the principle stands. Once the idea of neural plasticity is understood, it is then possible for learners to begin the process of shifting their mindsets. They begin to understand that the brain is actually growing and strengthening connections. It becomes clear that a growth mindset is not just a theory, but a truth.

Growth mindset study 2: the power of praise

Dweck and her colleagues also studied how mindsets are transmitted. In particular, in one famous study[6] she explored how praise transmits mindset messages to children.

In the first part of the study, children were all given a non-verbal IQ test. The test was matched to their age and aptitude, so most of the children got good scores on the test. Following the results, the children got three types of feedback:

1. Intelligence-focused feedback: "that's a really good score; you must be really smart at this."

2. Process-focused feedback: "that's a really good score; you must have tried really hard."

3. Neutral feedback: "that's a really good score."

The key to this experiment was the message transmitted through the feedback about what the adult valued in the child's success. In the first type of feedback, the message was that the adult valued intelligence or ability. It implied that the child was successful because of their innate talent, or that they were naturally good at these kinds of puzzles. In the second type of feedback, the message was that the adult valued the process that allowed the child to arrive at their success: their strategies for solving the problems, their effort, their focus, their persistence. The neutral feedback formed the control group: their success was noted, but not attributed to any particular quality.

Dweck and her team then began to explore the impact that the different types of praise had on the children in subsequent phases of the experiment. First, they offered the children a choice of a more difficult test, where they were likely to make mistakes but would certainly learn from the experience, or a test very similar to the one they had just done in which they would surely be successful. The results were astonishing. Over two-thirds of the children who had been praised for their intelligence opted for the easier option, whilst over 90 per cent of the children who had been praised for their process opted for the more challenging test.

Why might this be? Could such a subtle distinction in language really cause such a wide variation in the willingness of children to take on challenges? Dweck's supposition is that the messages within the feedback created mindset conditions in the children. When praised for their intelligence – "you must be so smart at this" – the children heard "the grown-up thinks I'm talented. That's why they admire me, that's why they value me." Therefore, when faced with a choice between a test in which they might make mistakes or one in which they would surely get a high score, they opted for the latter. It would maintain the image of intelligence which had garnered the praise from the adult in the earlier round of the experiment. The children had entered a fixed mindset, and their goal was performance-focused: to get a high score and to look smart at all costs.

By contrast, the children who had been told "you must have tried really hard at this" heard that the adult valued the process that they went through, the strategies they were using, and the fact that they were taking on a challenge. When they were faced with the same choice, they were willing to take on the harder challenge because trying something difficult was what had got them the praise in the earlier round. These children had entered a growth mindset. If they made a mistake on the hard task, they didn't worry that the adult wouldn't think they were talented. Rather, Dweck suggests, if they didn't take on the more difficult challenge, they would miss an opportunity to grow and the adult would be disappointed in them.

The experiment wasn't finished there, either. In the third round, all the students were given a very difficult set of non-verbal problems to solve. They were above the children's age and aptitude levels. The children were certain to find it a very difficult, even impossible, challenge. Again, the results were fascinating. The intelligence-praised fixed mindset children lost their confidence and gave up easily, frustrated by the difficulties they were faced with. The process-praised growth mindset children worked harder and longer at the difficult problems, even when they found them impossible to solve. Rather than being frustrated, many of them said that the harder problems were their favourite. They actually enjoyed them more!

In the final phase, the children were given a final non-verbal test at the same level as the first test they had been given. The fixed mindset group performed less well than they had the first time, whilst the growth mindset group increased their score by up to 30 per cent. Engaging with the process, taking on a more difficult challenge in the second round, and working harder and longer at the almost impossible challenges in round three had secured improvements in the children's ability to solve the non-verbal problems. The children who had coasted at the same level in the second round and given up quickly in the third round had squandered opportunities to learn and grow, and the damage to their confidence reduced their ability to complete problems that they had been able to solve earlier.

Implications for practice

The implications of Dweck's research into the effects of praise are far reaching. How often have we praised children in our own classes (or even our own children!)

for their natural abilities? How often have we told children that they are "gifted" or "talented"? How often have we told them how clever they are? Dweck's study shows us that this type of praise, though well intentioned, is actually damaging children's ability to learn by switching them off to learning.

Within a growth mindset school, we need to pay close attention to the language we are using not just to praise, but in all our interactions. Above all, we need to listen to the subtext of the language we are using and what it is implying. Our feedback should at all times carry the message that we value process, strategy, effort, focus and persistence. We should avoid phrases that suggest we value intelligence or natural ability.

Notes

1 Dweck, *Mindset.*
2 Ibid., page 6.
3 Sagan, *Broca's brain*, page 14.
4 Wiliam, "Becoming a better teacher."
5 Blackwell, Dweck, & Trzesniewski, "Implicit theories of intelligence predict achievement across an adolescent transition."
6 Mueller & Dweck, "Praise for intelligence can undermine children's motivation and performance."

Bibliography

Blackwell, L. S., Dweck, C. S., & Trzesniewski, K. (2007). Implicit theories of intelligence predict achievement across an adolescent transition: A longditudinal study and an intervention. *Child Development, 78*(1), 246–263.

Dweck, C. (2012). *Mindset: How you can fulfil your potential.* London: Robinson.

Mueller, C. M., & Dweck, C. S. (1998). Praise for intelligence can undermine children's motivation and performance. *Journal of Personality and Social Psychology, 75*(1), 33–52.

Sagan, C. (1979). *Broca's brain: Reflections on the romance of science.* London: Random House.

Wiliam, D. (n.d.) Becoming a better teacher – teachers doing it for themselves. Retrieved from Dylan Wiliam's blog: https://huntingenglish.wordpress.com/2013/06/15/becoming-a-better-teacher-teachers-doing-it-for-themselves/

2 Character education

I showed in Chapter 1 how growth mindset is rooted in extensive research undertaken by Dweck and others, with clear implications for teachers, schools, students, and families. By shifting the way we think about intelligence and ability, we can increase our achievement and feel more in control of our own destiny. We can transmit this mindset through the way we praise children, but also by the way we think about the structures, processes, and approaches we use in learning and development. In short, I would like to propose that schooling and education should be as much about *how* we teach students to tackle learning as it is about *what* we teach them. It is about building their character as much as about building their academic achievement. In this chapter, I will explore the debate about whether schools should be interfering in the character of the young people in their care and describe two complementary approaches which support the development of a growth mindset. Finally, I will outline the national policy context for becoming a growth mindset school, which comes under the banner of character education.

Should we be teaching character?

Before we progress to how we develop a growth mindset in our schools, it's worth considering whether we should be doing so at all – or even if we can. The first issue – whether we should be teaching character – comes down to a definition of what we mean by "character" in the first place. The dictionary definition is "the mental and moral qualities distinctive to an individual."[1] In this definition, teaching character could be seen as an attempt at personality modification, a mission to change the fundamental elements that make each individual unique. At its extreme, of course, it could be seen as an Orwellian attempt to homogenise society and as an attack on individuality. Naturally, this is not the approach that I will be advocating in these pages. I want to make the distinction between personality ("the combination of characteristics or qualities that form an individual's distinctive character"[2]) and those characteristics which enable students to be better learners.

I do not advocate that we attempt to change children's personalities. Any such move would, quite rightly, be met with staunch opposition from families and, I am certain, from the children themselves. Their uniqueness, variability, and quirky individuality are what make working with them such a joy. What I am suggesting instead is that we work to develop those qualities in them which will provide additional traction when it comes to academic and personal achievement. Such qualities identified by Dweck's research include the reaction to setbacks and failures, the approach to challenges, the attitude and belief relating to effort and talent, and the response to the success of others. Character education, in this context, is not an attempt to change a child's nature, but to change what they believe about themselves. No matter what their individual personality, character education can provide young people with approaches and strategies which can help them to persist when they struggle. When they do this, they should experience the virtuous circle of effort leading to success, which reinforces the need to apply effort in order to succeed in future. This is about giving children techniques which work, not about changing who they are.

For this reason, I do not propose decontextualised teaching of "character." The thought of timetabled lessons for "character building" is unpalatable to me. The primary function of the curriculum is to help students to progress in the matters, skills and processes they are learning, ensuring that they engage with "the best that has been thought and said"[3] to help them understand the world around them and make up their minds for themselves, critically and independently, about the issues which face them. Taking time and energy away from these things to develop a bespoke "character curriculum" would, I think, be a retrograde step and could encounter all the problems of transference that other "learning to learn" approaches have suffered from. Character education is about providing students with the skills, attitudes, beliefs, and techniques they need to be able to acquire curriculum knowledge most effectively, and to continue to learn beyond the time they spend in school. I believe that the approach to developing a growth mindset in our young people should be threaded through every interaction, every learning experience and every step on their educational journey. It should be a cultural expectation in our schools and beyond. As NFL linebacker Ray Lewis says, "greatness is a lot of small things done well."

The thornier issue, perhaps, is whether we *can* teach character in this way. Surely "character" is inherited, a product of nature not nurture? At the very least, isn't the "character" our students display formed by the home environment long before they come to school? Research certainly indicates that large aspects of our characters and personalities are inherited. If our parents have a great deal of persistence and resilience, it is likely that we will too. If they give up easily, become frustrated, and are prone to anger, then it is likely that we will inherit those qualities through a combination of genetic inheritance and environmental conditioning. Surely then, if children's personalities are already formed by their genetic composition and environment before they even set foot inside a school, character education is a fruitless endeavour?

It is, of course, more complex than that. Most estimates put the heritability of personality traits at a mean of about 0.5,[4] meaning that about half of our observable personality traits are written into our genes, whilst the other half are subject to environmental factors. But, crucially, our characters are not fixed but continue to change and develop throughout our lives, especially through adolescence and into early adulthood.[5] Just because we are prone to hot-headedness and anger in youth, does not mean that we are sentenced for life to short-tempered outbursts. We can learn and, through learning, change our behaviour. We can learn to become more tolerant of others; we can learn to share; we can learn to persevere. A 2012 study entitled "Can an old dog learn (and want to experience) new tricks?"[6] found that openness to new experiences could be improved in older adults through a cognitive training programme. In fact, our character traits, like our intelligence and our ability, are not fixed constructs.

A further issue with the argument that students' characters are already pre-formed before they arrive at school is related to the fact that nobody has any issue with schools working flat out to modify unacceptable social behaviours such as violence, verbal abuse, or vandalism. These behaviours are just as much part of individual students' characters as any other. Working in schools, we know those students who arrive with us with a tendency to lash out, a disregard for authority and a predilection to cause damage, and we are onto them quickly, working hard to modify their behaviour through a combination of reward, sanction and carefully targeted coaching and instruction. We involve the families, who may or may not be supportive. We may involve external professionals – psychologists, therapists, even the police. All of these efforts are made with the intention of curbing the tendencies of the child that we in schools, and society at large, find unacceptable. Of course, we don't always succeed. But sometimes we do. Sometimes, with the right intervention at the right time, the right support, the right conditions, we get through to children. They see sense. They *want* to change, and they invest their effort and their will into making that change. They may have a lapse as they try to turn things around, but we are patient with them. We know that changing habits is hard, so we give them a chance. We give them time. And when they leave school in Year 11, they look back at the behaviour record of the Year 8 that they were and they can't believe it's the same person.

I am proposing that we exert the same kinds of influences over poor learning behaviours as we do over poor social behaviours. Avoiding challenging tasks, giving up easily, refusing to try, ignoring or refusing to act on useful feedback – these should be just as unacceptable to professionals in the education sector as swearing, hitting, or kicking; and we should marshal our energies to tackle them. Just as with social behaviours, we need to be patient, kind, and completely consistent in our expectations. We may need the help of other professionals. We will certainly need the support of the family – more on this in Chapter 12. But above all, we need to convince the children themselves of the need to change, so that they will invest their effort, time, and willpower into the challenging task of habit change. What I am proposing in becoming a growth mindset school is not that our institutions become mechanisms for personality transplant, but that we engage in working with young people to help them acquire the skills and dispositions which enable them to be successful learners in the future. If we focus on the attitudes and beliefs with which our students approach their learning, we could transform their ability to access, retain and use that learning.

What marshmallows can teach us about self-control

Walter Mischel is one of the modern pioneers of research into the psychology of motivation and willpower. In the 1960s, Mischel and his students undertook a study with preschool children at Stanford University's Bing Nursery School. The preschoolers were offered the choice of one reward (most famously, a marshmallow, although Mischel and his team did use other treats) which they could have immediately or a larger reward (for example, two marshmallows) later on. In order to receive the larger reward, the children would have to wait, alone, with the single marshmallow in front of them, resisting the temptation to eat it in the knowledge that their willpower would bring double the reward later. Mischel's study was focused on the techniques and strategies that the preschoolers used in order to delay gratification, but what he and his students were not prepared for was the way in which performance on the marshmallow test predicted success and achievement in later life. In his book *The Marshmallow Test*,[7] Mischel shows how those preschoolers who were able to delay gratification for longer in the study went on to score higher on their college admission SATs, developed higher social and cognitive functions, and had a greater sense of self-worth as adults. He even found correlations between delaying gratification and lower body mass index, and differences in brain functions linked to addiction and obesity. Essentially, Mischel suggests, the ability to exercise willpower in early childhood is an excellent predictor of who will be a well-adjusted, successful adult. It is easy to see the links between willpower and study: those students who are likely to be most successful academically will be those who are able to resist the temptations of the games console, the black mirror of the smartphone, and the lure of social media in exchange for the textbook, revision notes, and retrieval practice that they know is necessary to enable their long-term success.

Mischel has devoted much of his career since those early studies to understanding how and why willpower works. He concludes that there are two different systems operating in the brain when it comes to resisting temptation: a "hot" system and a "cool" system. The "hot" limbic system is an evolutionary hangover from our earliest hunter-gatherer ancestors, an instinctive and primal function which could perhaps be characterised as our Mr Hyde, or our Freudian id. Situated under the cortex at the top of our brain stem, and particularly focused on the tiny almond-shaped amygdala, the limbic system motivates us to immediate action. It responds quickly to strong stimuli around fear, pleasure and pain. As *homo erectus*, our limbic system would have enabled the fight or flight impulses that allowed early humankind to escape sabre-toothed tigers, to breed, and to eat. When faced with the temptation of a soft, sweet marshmallow, our limbic system is crying out, "eat it now!"

Resisting these "hot" impulses is the "cool" cognitive system, primarily situated in the prefrontal cortex of the brain. The "cool" system develops slowly as we grow up. Infants are completely governed by their limbic systems, crying out when cold, hungry, tired or frightened. Over time, children learn to control those impulsive behaviours which interfere with long-term goals, regulating their behaviour and allowing the kind of "self-talk" which Dweck advocates when encouraging us to invoke our "growth mindset voice" in response to fixed mindset thinking. For example, when we encounter difficulty or failure, our "hot" limbic system will encourage us to give up, wail, gnash our teeth, and weep. Our "cool" cognitive system will allow us to control those impulses, take a deep breath, and remind ourselves that "mistakes are great, they help us learn" before we pick ourselves up to have another go. In the marshmallow test, the "cool" system allows subjects to control the temptation to eat the single marshmallow in the knowledge that there is a future, currently unseen, reward of two marshmallows ahead.

In the marshmallow test studies, Mischel and his colleagues found a correlation between those subjects who were able to delay gratification for the longest in preschool and those who went on to be successful adults according to a range of different metrics. Whilst this may be of great interest, it is not significant unless we can in some way influence the exercise of the "cool" system to control the impulses of the "hot" system in the brains of our students. It may just be that some people are born with a greater predisposition towards self-control and that it is a heritable feature of our character. However, Mischel's conclusions about the nature vs nurture debate in relation to the exercise of willpower are significant. He argues that whilst an individual's predispositions and characteristics are inherited genetically, the environment within which an individual grows up can and does influence the extent and manner to which their genes are expressed. He cites experiments with mice in laboratories, where strains of mice were bred to be genetically shy (BALB mice) or genetically fearless (B6 mice). When infant B6 mice were placed with BALB mothers, their fearlessness receded and their timidity increased.[8] In other words, their environment influenced the way in which their genetic composition was expressed. The significant generational gains in IQ witnessed in developed countries over the past century are too rapid to be evolutionary so, according to psychologist James R. Flynn,[9] they are instead likely to be evidence of our environment influencing the expression of our genetic code, "switching on" aspects of our DNA related to intelligence. In other words, a genetic predisposition is not the same as a predetermination. If we are born predisposed to lack self-control and willpower, this does not mean that we are unable to learn it.

Mischel's studies are of particular relevance when thinking about building a growth mindset culture in a school. The teaching of self-control and ability to exercise willpower is an essential part of developing and maintaining a growth mindset. Mischel identified the significant strategies that his test subjects used when delaying gratification in the marshmallow test. They included distraction and abstraction: either taking your mind off the temptation altogether by thinking about something else or turning the temptation into an abstract concept such as a picture or a model. By focusing on representing the temptation using "cool" cognitive functions – for example, thinking about how the marshmallow is similar to a cloud, as it is white and puffy – Mischel's subjects were able to delay gratification for up to 17 minutes, whereas those not provided with strategies were only able to wait for around 6 minutes. Equally, when test subjects were able to visualise the longer-term goal (two marshmallows), they were able to delay gratification for longer. Vitally, when Mischel and his researchers *taught* the test subjects to use those strategies, even subjects with previously low willpower found that they were able to delay gratification for longer. In other words, children can get better at exercising self-control and delaying gratification if they are provided with the techniques and strategies (and the right conditions) to do so. In just the same way as Dweck found that teaching children about how the brain learns could change their mindsets, Mischel has found that our capacity to exercise willpower and self-control is malleable. The interplay of these qualities and approaches is fundamental to developing a growth mindset culture in schools.

Getting gritty about getting our kids grittier

In 2007, Angela Duckworth and colleagues published their seminal paper on the topic of grit.[10] Duckworth and her team had studied students at elite universities, cadets at West Point military academy, and contestants at the Scripps National Spelling Bee, with the aim of working out which individuals were successful in these challenging situations and why they were successful. In their studies, they found that a quality called "grit" was a greater determiner of success in these varied and challenging environments than IQ, social intelligence, or even conscientiousness. Duckworth defines grit as "perseverance and passion for long-term goals,"[11] and her contention is that higher ratings on her "grit scale" serve to explain why some individuals achieve more than others of equal intelligence. She suggests that "the achievement of difficult goals entails not only talent but also the sustained and focused application of talent over time."[12]

Duckworth's work had been prompted by her experiences of teaching Maths in New York public schools, where she noticed a disparity between the IQ scores of her class and their performances on her tests and quizzes. She saw that some of the smartest students in her classes – those with higher IQ scores – were being outscored by those with lower IQ scores. Clearly, there was something else at work, other than IQ, in predicting academic success. She was also convinced that the concepts of mathematics she was teaching were not beyond the reach of any of her students and that, if they worked hard and long enough, every single student in her class should be capable of mastering them. And so, having already left her job as a high-flying McKinsey consultant, she left teaching and devoted her career to identifying this X-factor component of success – grit.

The interrelation of grit with Mischel's work on willpower is clear. In order to sustain focus on a long-term goal, whether that is academic success, sporting achievement, or attaining a competitive edge in any other field, individuals must defer gratification and sustain motivation in the face of struggle, challenge, and difficulty in pursuit of the goal. They have to keep going when others would give up. They have to have the same attitude as Grammy-award-winning musician and Oscar-nominated actor Will Smith, who is quoted in Duckworth's book:

> The only thing I see that is distinctly different about me is: I'm not afraid to die on a treadmill. I will not be outworked, period. You might have more talent than me, you might be smarter than me, you might be sexier than me. You might be all of those things. You got it on me in nine categories. But if we get on the treadmill together, there's two things: you're getting off first, or I'm going to die. It's really that simple.[13]

Grit enables individuals to maximise their talent and turn it into achievement. Duckworth renders the relationship between talent and achievement mathematically as follows:

talent × *effort* = skill

skill × *effort* = achievement

She explains: "talent is how quickly your skills improve when you invest effort. Achievement is what happens when you take your acquired skills and use them."[14] It is grit that enables successful individuals to undertake the sustained deliberate practice necessary to improve a skill to the point of expertise – the fabled 10,000 hours cited by Malcolm Gladwell[15] and expanded by Matthew Syed[16] and others. And just as Dweck concludes with mindset, and Mischel with self-control and willpower, Duckworth's research shows that whilst heritability accounts for some of our grittiness, grit is not a fixed construct – it can grow. The interplay of nature and nurture can enable individuals to develop their grittiness. And Duckworth codifies how individuals can become grittier into four factors: interest, practice, purpose, and hope.

Interest is vital because it enables us to stay the course – we need to love what we are doing if we are to persevere. We are fortunate, particularly in secondary schools, in that teachers are those who are so enthusiastic about their subjects that they have devoted their careers to passing that interest on. In schools, the subjects we teach all have an inherent interest level built into them, and teachers can unlock that interest in the students they teach. Practice, as we have already seen, is essential to turn talent into skill and skill into achievement. Purpose is giving students a sense that what they are learning about, or learning how to do, *matters*. That it is going to make a difference. Not necessarily in a utilitarian "I need to know this in order to survive as a functioning adult" kind of way, but in the sense that there is a bigger picture to what they are learning – a sense that this lesson is part of an overall construct that will enrich and enable them. And finally, hope – the sense that no matter how difficult and challenging things might seem, they can be overcome; the sense that success is possible; the unshakeable belief that we *can* get there if we keep going. This is not the blind hope of just imagining that tomorrow will somehow be better than today, but taking action to ensure that tomorrow will be better. In the words of Thomas Edison: "our greatest weakness lies in giving up. The most certain way to succeed is always to try just one more time."

In our schools, we can control those variables. Our interactions with our students can awaken and sustain interest in the material we are teaching. Our curriculum design can systematise the need for practice and ensure that it is purposeful and beneficial. Our vision for education, developing our young people into learners within and beyond our schools, can provide education with a purpose which the learners can share. And our unconditional positive regard for those young people, and our encouragement and insistence and consistent practice of the audacity of hope, can create a culture in which grit, self-control, and the growth mindset can flourish.

Character education policy

In June 2015, the then Education Secretary, Nicky Morgan MP, addressed the Sunday Times Festival of Education at Wellington College. Her topic was no less than "the future of education in England," and one of the key threads she picked up in that speech was the importance of character education. In a section of the speech headed "Creating the conditions for success," Morgan said:

> we know that children need certain character traits to excel academically. The kind of traits that should be embedded through a whole-school approach to character education, helping children and young people become decent, happy, well-balanced citizens.
>
> [. . .] Building a strong character and a sense of moral purpose is part of the responsibility we have towards our children, our society and our nation. Because if our schools don't nurture and develop these key traits, we run the risk of creating a generation who excel at passing exams, writing essays, absorbing information, but children without the skills they need to tackle the

challenges that lie ahead and participate in society as active citizens, to make the right decisions and build their own moral framework.[17]

Morgan went on to suggest that the school curriculum should include character education, including *"the growth mindset*, the ability to deal with set-backs, and the willingness to practice"* (my italics).

As a policy directive, Morgan was clearly building on the weight of evidence sitting behind the approaches to learning, citing Doug Lemov and Matthew Syed in her speech alongside Dweck's work. It was a theme she returned to throughout her time as Secretary of State, launching the Character Awards in 2015 to recognise schools "leading the field in character education," which help to teach students:

- how to persevere and work to achieve

- . . . how to bounce back if faced with failure[18]

Speaking at the opening of a "character symposium" in January 2016, Morgan began to explore the link between character education and mental health, citing her appointment of Sam Gyimah as the first minister with a specific remit for mental health. She reiterated her support for the research carried out by Dweck and others:

> we're not promoting character on a whim. Evidence clearly shows that character matters. Carole [sic] Dweck's work at Stanford, Angela Duckworth's work on Character Lab, as well as the evidence collected by the Early Intervention Foundation, all point to success being closely linked with character.
>
> [. . .] One of the other myths I'm keen to dispel is that character education, and academic attainment are mutually exclusive. Far from it. For me, they are 2 sides of the same coin. Consider for a moment the student who reads aloud for the first time and gets tongue tied – will they rush to do it again without encouragement? What about another who is asked to recite times tables in front of their class and gets stuck – will they fall over themselves to repeat the exercise? Probably not. But with character comes the confidence and determination not to be beaten. It's that attitude that says "dust yourself off and try again."[19]

Morgan's words became policy in the 2016 White Paper *Educational Excellence Everywhere*, which contained a section on "Building character and resilience in every child":

> A 21st century education should prepare children for adult life by instilling the character traits . . . that will help them succeed: being resilient and knowing how to persevere, how to bounce back if faced with failure, and how to collaborate with others at work and in their private lives.[20]

The White Paper goes on again to suggest a link between character education and good mental health, noting that "schools can play an important role in promoting wellbeing as well as helping to prevent and identify mental health issues."[21] Morgan's ongoing commitment to character education was emphasised when the awards she had initiated in 2015 were accompanied by £6 million of funding for "character grants" to develop and share best practice, announced in May 2016.[22]

For a time at least, it seemed as though there was a significant policy drive towards recognising the kinds of approaches that Dweck's research had been promoting, accompanied by funding to support it and a sense that schools which developed these attributes and dispositions would be recognised and celebrated. Whilst my views diverge from Nicky Morgan's on many issues, on this one I was happy to endorse her. But, as is so often the way, politics intervened. A staunch "remain" campaigner in the EU referendum, Morgan threw her hat into the ring as a potential Conservative Party leadership candidate following David Cameron's resignation in the wake of the vote to leave. She then gave her support to prominent "leave" campaigner and former Education Secretary Michael Gove, whose bid for the leadership ended in failure. Theresa May, the successful candidate, on her first day as Prime Minister, removed Nicky Morgan from office. Her successor, Justine Greening, made no mention of character education in her inaugural speech. The character grants were awarded in June 2016, with £2 million of the funding going to projects which had a "military ethos approach to develop character."[23] They have not been renewed. The character awards have been discontinued.

The subsequent Green Paper issued under Prime Minister Theresa May and Education Secretary Justine Greening, entitled *Schools that Work for Everyone*,[24] made no mention of the character initiatives. In place of the emphasis on character came, instead, a proposal to lift the ban on new grammar schools, which select students based on educational ability. There are many things to take issue with in this policy, and one of them is the threat that selection poses to the development of growth mindset approaches to education. Of the top-performing school systems internationally, surveyed by Lucy Crehan in her excellent book *Cleverlands*, Finland, Japan, and Canada all operate fully comprehensive systems up to the end of secondary school, having moved away from selection to improve both equity and equality within their schools. Only Singapore operates a selective system, and as Crehan explains, this leads to families taking leave from work to coach their children through the Primary School Leaving Examination (or PSLE), paying for private tuition, and heaping excessive pressure onto young children to perform in a one-off, high-stakes test at age 12. Crehan also eloquently points out that the premise of the selective system operating in Singapore is based on an "outdated and inaccurate understanding of intelligence"[25] that suggests a test at age 12 will identify "able" or "intelligent" children and act as a reliable predictor of academic potential. This belief – that you only get a set amount of "ability" or "intelligence" which is defined by heritability and which does not change over time – is the definition of the fixed mindset.

The proposal to allow the expansion of selection at age 11 in England therefore ran completely counter to the development of growth mindsets in our young people. In its simplest form, a growth mindset is the belief that your intelligence and ability can grow over time. We know that children develop at different rates and that whilst some will excel in primary, some will only flourish towards the end of secondary school. Current thinking suggests that intelligence develops and improves in surges, rather like growth spurts.[26] Labelling children either "can" or "cannot" at the end of primary school clearly creates a problem for those many children who "fail" the 11 plus. How are we to help them believe that they can achieve and learn and grow when the test which meant they ended up in your school, rather than the one they wanted to go to, acts as a permanent marker and reminder of the fact that they have already failed? Quite aside from the fact that grammar schools – like the selective schools in Singapore – are predominantly the domain of those wealthy enough to be able to pay for extra tuition and whose family backgrounds provide the kind of academic support required to succeed in the test, the very notion of streaming students in this way acts as a brake on the positive self-belief of the majority. To become a growth mindset school, the school needs to teach a challenging and demanding curriculum to *all* children, not just the few, assisted by a culture predicated on the belief that *all* children, not just the few, can achieve.

I am used, by now, to the vicissitudes of education policy and the fluctuations that occur as successive Secretaries of State use their office to advance their own particular agendas. Under Nicky Morgan, there was a sense of alignment between policy and evidence-based practice that seemed to offer a positive way forward for developing growth mindset approaches in UK schools, supported by funding. In the political turmoil that followed the EU referendum, that momentum was lost and replaced by a policy position that seemed predicated, instead, on fixed mindset thinking; that too was further consumed by the hung parliament following the snap general election in 2017 and the shelving – for now – of the proposal to further extend selection. It is my hope that despite changes in policy direction from central government, schools and school leaders will continue to define the ethos and approach of their own institutions to developing character.

Notes

1 Pearsall, *Concise Oxford Dictionary*.
2 Ibid.
3 Matthew Arnold's definition of culture, from his preface to *Culture and Anarchy*.
4 For example, Harkness & Lilienfield, "Individual differences science for treatment planning."
5 Roberts, Wood, & Caspi, "The development of personality traits in adulthood."
6 Jackson, Hill, Payne, Roberts, & Stine-Morrow, "Can an old dog learn (and want to experience) new tricks?"
7 Mischel, *The Marshmallow Test*.
8 Mischel is referring to: D.D. Francis et al. (2003). "Epigenetic sources of behavioural differences in mice," *Nature Neuroscience*, 6(5), 445–446.
9 Flynn (1987) "Massive IQ gains in 14 nations: What IQ tests really measure."

10 Duckworth, Peterson, Matthews, & Kelly, "Grit."
11 Ibid., page 1087.
12 Ibid.
13 Will Smith, quoted in Duckworth, *Grit*, page 46.
14 Ibid., page 42.
15 Gladwell, *Outliers.*
16 For example, in *Bounce.*
17 Morgan, "Nicky Morgan discusses the future of education in England."
18 The awards ran for two years: https://www.gov.uk/government/news/awards-launched-for-schools-best-at-instilling-character
19 Morgan, "Nicky Morgan opens character symposium at Floreat School."
20 Department for Education, *Educational Excellence Everywhere*, section 6.33.
21 Ibid., section 6.42.
22 Morgan, "Funding boost for schools helping pupils develop character."
23 Whittaker, "£2m 'character education' grant goes to military-style projects."
24 Department for Education, *Schools that Work for Everyone.*
25 Crehan, *Cleverlands*, page 111.
26 Ibid., page 116.

Bibliography

Arnold, M. (2015). *Culture and Anarchy and Other Selected Prose.* London: Penguin Classics.

Crehan, L. (2016). *Cleverlands.* London: Unbound.

Department for Education. (2016, 12 April). Awards launched for schools best at instilling character. Retrieved 11 April, 2017, from *GOV.UK*: https://www.gov.uk/government/news/awards-launched-for-schools-best-at-instilling-character

Department for Education. (2016). *Educational Excellence Everywhere.* London: Department for Education.

Department for Education. (2016, 12 September). *Schools that Work for Everyone: Government Consultation.* London: Department for Education.

Duckworth, A. (2016). *Grit.* London: Vermilion.

Duckworth, A. L., Peterson, C., Matthews, M. D., & Kelly, D. R. (2007). Grit: Perseverance and passion for long-term goals. *Journal of Personality and Social Psychology, 92*(6), 1087–1101.

Flynn, J. R. (1987). Massive IQ gains in 14 nations: What IQ tests really measure. *Psychological Bulletin, 101*(2), 171–191.

Gladwell, M. (2009). *Outliers.* London: Penguin.

Harkness, A. R., & Lilienfield, S. O. (1997). Individual differences science for treatment planning: Personality traits. *Psychological Assessment, 9*(4), 349–360.

Harris, J. R. (2009). *The Nurture Assumption: Why Children Turn Out the Way They Do.* New York: Free Press.

Jackson, J. J., Hill, P. L., Payne, B. R., Roberts, B. W., & Stine-Morrow, E. A. (2012, June). Can an old dog learn (and want to experience) new tricks? Cognitive training increases openness to experience in older adults. *Psychology and Aging, 27*(2), 286–292.

Mischel, W. (2015). *The Marshmallow Test.* London: Transworld Publishers.

Morgan, N. (2015, 18 June). Nicky Morgan discusses the future of education in England. Retrieved 11 April, 2017, from *GOV.UK*: https://www.gov.uk/government/speeches/nicky-morgan-discusses-the-future-of-education-in-england

Morgan, N. (2016, 21 January). Nicky Morgan opens character symposium at Floreat School. Retrieved 11 April, 2017, from *GOV.UK*: https://www.gov.uk/government/speeches/nicky-morgan-opens-character-symposium-at-floreat-school

Morgan, N. (2016, 23 February). Nicky Morgan: A world-class education system for every child. Retrieved 11 April, 2017, from *GOV.UK*: https://www.gov.uk/government/speeches/a-world-class-education-system-for-every-child

Morgan, N. (2016, 26 May). Funding boost for schools helping pupils develop character [press release]. Retrieved 1 November, 2017, from *GOV.UK*: https://www.gov.uk/government/news/funding-boost-for-schools-helping-pupils-develop-character

North, A. (2015, 10 January). Should schools teach personality? *The New York Times*.

Pearsall, J. (1999). *The Concise Oxford Dictionary* (10th edition). Oxford: Oxford University Press.

Roberts, B.W., Wood, D., & Caspi, A. (2010). The development of personality traits in adulthood. In O.P. John, R.P. Robins, & L.P. Pervi (eds), *Handbook of Personality: Theory and Research* (pp. 375–398). New York: Guildford Press.

Syed, M. (2011). *Bounce.* London: Fourth Estate.

Whittaker, F. (2016, 26 June). £2m "character education" grant goes to military-style projects. Retrieved 11 April, 2017, from *Schools Week*: http://schoolsweek.co.uk/2m-more-earmarked-for-military-style-projects/

Young, T. (2014, 8 November). Why schools can't teach character. *The Spectator*.

3 Why growth mindset?

As I was reading *Mindset* and the research behind it, broadening my knowledge by exploring Walter Mischel's and Angela Duckworth's books and research, and seeing the overlap with Matthew Syed's *Bounce*, I found myself nodding along. These books and the psychology they were exploring uncovered a half-realised truth, articulating something that I felt I had always known but not understood. It was as if the researchers had managed to pull off that fundamental teaching trick of making the implicit explicit. I was interested in my own reaction to this research, and I was nervous about it too. If something seems too good to be true, it usually is. Was I at risk of falling for a fad?

I reflected on my own experience of education and how it had led me up to this point. I had always been academically successful, from primary school onwards. I enjoyed my primary education at the local school. I mainly remember playing with toy cars, keeping an apple core in my flip-top desk to see how much it would shrivel up, and collecting the stubs of used-up pencils in an old tobacco tin. But I also remember a few moments from lessons which stand out. What could these tell me about my mindset?

My earliest memory of learning something new at school involved the number 9. This must have been very early in the infants, although I can't remember exactly how old I was at the time. What I do remember is that the class was split into teams and we had to write figures on the board in chalk. The teams earned points for forming the letters correctly. I had to write the number 9, which I did, exactly as I'd been taught it, with a circle on the top and a curling tail, a bit like a lower-case "g." My team were frantic – "Not like that!" "That's wrong!" "It needs a straight line!" I couldn't understand them. I knew that I was right. I was convinced of it. And I held my nerve. As we revealed the figures on the board, I saw with a sinking heart that the opposing team had written the 9 with a straight line, like a mirror-image letter "p." Had I been wrong all this time? Had I let my team down in the game?

The teacher came to my rescue, explaining to the class that there were two ways to write the number 9 and that my way was just as right as the other way. This was amazing to them – and to me. Two different ways to write the same number – both of them correct? It was as though vistas of possibility had opened up before us. It's the first time that I remember explicitly learning something specific, and this stuck with me. From that point on, I switched the way I wrote "9" from my way to the other way and back again. The fact that both could be correct fascinated me, and I wanted to push at that boundary.

Why did this experience stick with me, and what can it tell us about mindset? First, it was an experience forged in the heat of competition and pressure. I felt, possibly for the first time, the weight of responsibility to my team. I had to make a call, either to stick with what I thought was right or to switch to what my team was telling me. I stuck to my guns. I remember feeling confident in my answer, but not unshakeably so. Above all, though, I remember the rush of pride in feeling vindicated and the wonder that there were two possible answers to the problem.

I am sure that the pressure of the situation helped to form the memory so firmly in my mind. But also I think this memory shows how learning can be reinforced by the feeling of achievement and success. I had to really think, really try, and the effort was rewarded with success. This experience reinforced a connection in my mind that equated effort and determination with that really, really good feeling – the dopamine shot of success.

I also remember my lessons with Mr Jones, probably at the start of what is now Key Stage 2. For Maths, Mr Jones was keen on competition too, and the programme of study consisted of books with titles like *Five A Day*, *Six A Day*, *Seven A Day*, *Eight A Day*, and so on. They did what they said on the cover: they were books full of sets of maths problems designed to be completed over the course of a school year. The problems got successively more difficult through the books. We had heard tell in playground legend of big boys and girls who were halfway through *Twelve A Day*, but we were mostly convinced that this was a myth. Such an achievement could not be possible . . . could it?

Mr Jones set aside a portion of each day for us to work on our *Six A Day* books. We had to get them all right before we could move on to the next one. Any errors and we had to write out the correction before we moved on. I don't know whether he set it up as a competition, but I do know that the children in his class made it one. We pushed one another to do better, motivated to beat one another. Our positions in the hierarchy changed daily as we strove to outdo each other.

Reflecting on this process now, it seems to run the risk of setting up conditions similar to Dweck's sixth-grade teacher, Mrs Wilson, who sat all the children in IQ order – the risk of creating a fixed mindset hierarchy. What made this different, though, was that the competition was solely based on the effort and application that we put into solving the problems in our *Six A Day* books. And when my friend Ali moved on to *Seven A Day* before me, I was spurred into action. There were no shortcuts. I had to work harder, faster, and smarter to catch up. I kept on doing as much maths as I could in the allotted time, putting in the effort and seeing the reward as I conquered another set of problems so that I could move on to the next, harder, set. And so did Ali and Simon and Pamela and Karis and

Nicola and all the children on my table. We pushed ourselves, and each other, to continue to improve.

What became clear in Mr Jones' classroom was that pushing yourself to take on harder challenges was valued. In fact, it was expected. Whether by accident or design, Mr Jones had created the perfect conditions for a growth mindset to take root and to flourish. We understood that we had to put in the effort to continue to achieve, and to grasp, the maths that we were learning. We understood that we had to repeatedly practice the same operations to gain mastery of them. And we understood that there was always a harder challenge above the one that we were doing, so that when we raced through easier problems, it was always en route to something that would really make us think. And we loved it. I can remember to this day going through to the headteacher's office, my completed *Seven A Day* book clutched in my hands. The headteacher had an ottoman in the shape of a rhinoceros, which he'd brought back from Africa. He shook my hand. "On to *Eight A Day* now, then!" he said in his broad Welsh accent. I couldn't wait.

Is competition healthy?

Around me at this time, discussions were happening at home about which secondary school I should attend. I wasn't really aware of this at the time, but I've talked about it since to try and understand. Essentially, my parents saw that I was bright and hungry to learn, and they were worried that the local comprehensive wouldn't stretch and challenge me enough. They wanted the best for me, so they put me in for the entrance exam for an elitist, high-performing boys' independent school not too far from where we lived. I remember driving up to the school to sit the exam with my friend Simon, testing each other on capital cities of countries around the world. This didn't come up in the exam, but we knew a lot of them. I don't remember much about the exam itself, but I know that I got a bursary to attend the school. Every year my academic performance was monitored to make sure I was still eligible to receive this money. If I hadn't met the standard, my parents would no longer have been able to afford to send me there.

Looking back on this now with adult eyes, that seems like a lot of pressure to put on a child, but it didn't feel like it at the time. In reality, I had no concept of the financial and political decisions behind my education. As far as I was concerned, I was just going to school. One of my primary school friends came with me. The others didn't. It wasn't a big deal – on the first day of the first year hardly anyone knew anyone else, but we soon did. I made friends. I did well. That was all.

It's only with the benefit of hindsight that I can see how my secondary education was fundamentally different. Of course, there were the facilities and opportunities which come with a well-funded private school. But more than that, there was the implicit academic challenge of a selective education. We had passed an exam to be there. Within that environment, there was an expectation that we would push ourselves hard and achieve the very highest results. I don't remember this ever being explicit, but there was no doubt that it was there, especially in the fact that my continuing place at the school depended on my academic performance. I was very competitive, and I thrived on the challenge of trying to be the best that I could be. But whilst I was at secondary school, it also began to matter to me how good I was *compared to others*.

I think I can trace this back to the end of my first year, when I was awarded the end-of-year prizes for Science (Biology) and English. This meant that I had come top in the end-of-year exams. The rank order was published, so we could see where we came. It felt amazing. My parents, my whole family in fact, were bursting with pride. The prize-giving ceremony took place on 17 October, 1987, the day after the Great Storm battered the country. We had to make our way past felled trees and wind-ravaged buildings to get to the school at all. But I walked up on stage, shook the headteacher's hand, and collected my book prize.

This contact with the headteacher at my secondary school had a very different impact to sitting on the rhinoceros ottoman in Mr Jones' office at primary school. At primary, my achievement was the result of the application and effort that I'd put in relative only to myself. Anybody else who had finished their *Seven A Day* would have been rewarded in the same way. Anybody could achieve it, if only they worked hard enough. But now, at secondary, I was receiving the only prize for English that was on offer. It was only achievable by one person. And I had won it. In that moment, surrounded by storm damage and chaos, it felt amazing. But I never won it again. And at the end of the second year, when I came fifth in the year, I felt like a failure.

With the award of the English prize, a fixed mindset hierarchy had been created. From that point forward, I measured myself against the success of others, constantly looking over my shoulder at the competition – the epitome of a fixed mindset. It's no wonder that Carol Dweck's story about being sat around the room in IQ order by Mrs Wilson in sixth grade strikes such a chord with me! And this continued through school, right up to the very senior years. In the sixth form, school prizes were awarded for the highest-performing students across the whole year. I came second in English. And I was disappointed.

There is sufficient distance now for me to put this into context. By every logical metric, I had been hugely successful at school. I had a place to read English at Oxford; I got an A at A-Level and a 1 in S-Level English – but still I was disappointed, because there was someone better than me. It turns out the teachers were absolutely right: the prize was awarded to my contemporary Andrew Miller, who went on to write the Man Booker-nominated novel *Snowdrops*.[1] I should have been proud of my achievements, but I wasn't, and this was entirely due to the competitive ethos of my school, where only one person could feel truly proud of what they had achieved.

I still wrestle with this in my own mind. The school had established, within its own confines, a true meritocracy, and I wasn't good enough to win. It is entirely possible that without the competitive ethos, I would not have achieved as highly as I did. But in a growth mindset, we should be measuring performance against our own yardstick, aiming to better our own personal best irrespective of the performance of others. I did not have a frame of reference to manage this disappointment. In my fixed mindset, I was unable to learn from the experience, which left me bitter.

There is, of course, a growth mindset way to approach situations such as this. Carol Dweck gives the example of Elizabeth in *Mindset*, which is cited on her website:

> Nine-year-old Elizabeth was on her way to her first gymnastics meet. Lanky, flexible, and energetic, she was just right for gymnastics, and she loved it. Of course, she was a little nervous about competing, but she was good at gymnastics and felt confident of doing well. She had even thought about the perfect place in her room to hang the ribbon she would win.
>
> In the first event, the floor exercises, Elizabeth went first. Although she did a nice job, the scoring changed after the first few girls and she lost. Elizabeth also did well in the other events, but not well enough to win. By the end of the evening, she had received no ribbons and was devastated.
>
> What would you do if you were Elizabeth's parents?
>
> ■ Tell Elizabeth you thought she was the best.
>
> ■ Tell her she was robbed of a ribbon that was rightfully hers.
>
> ■ Reassure her that gymnastics is not that important.
>
> ■ Tell her she has the ability and will surely win next time.
>
> ■ Tell her she didn't deserve to win.[2]

I went through all of those responses in my own mind as I wrestled with the disappointment of coming second to Andrew Miller. I tried to convince myself that an injustice had been done and that I had been robbed of the prize that was rightfully mine. I went through the phase of telling myself that it didn't matter and that one prize was not that important. In the end, I had to face up to the hard truth that I didn't deserve to win. But at the time, I was in a fixed mindset about it, and that made it difficult to accept. The way I saw it, Andrew Miller was more talented than me. He was better than me. And there was nothing that I could do about it. The experience of coming second is one that has permeated through to my own teaching and school leadership.

Kellan's story

As a teacher, I have been inspired by students I have taught who had completely different beliefs about intelligence and ability to those I held in school. In particular, I remember Kellan. Kellan was a bright, creative, and sparky girl in my GCSE

Media Studies group. She had a healthy sense of irony and a sharp intellect, quick to make connections between ideas and able to see the bigger picture. She was a joy to teach. However, her confidence was fragile and she didn't see in herself the qualities that I was recognising. She lacked the belief that she was talented – that wasn't how she saw herself. I spent much of the year building her up, lavishing praise on her work, and watching her slowly begin to realise her potential. In the end-of-year exam halfway through the GCSE course, Kellan put a lot of time and effort into her preparations and produced a fantastic set of answers to the mock. She gave her ideas free rein, pushed herself, and drew together theory and content knowledge from across the year to excel. In fact, it was the best in the class by a clear five marks.

I've stayed in touch with Kellan, who is now at university studying English Literature with Creative Writing. I spoke to her about her experiences at school and about the interplay between hard work and natural ability. In our conversation, she explained that back in Year 7 she had won the school's Junior Spelling Bee competition. She still remembered the experience as a formative one. New to the school, with few friends of her own, she noticed that more and more supporters who had come along to cheer on their friends began to cheer for her as their friends were knocked out, until eventually she correctly spelled more words than any other student in her year group. This achievement marked her out as a high performer academically, and she found comfort in that reputation. Importantly, however, coming first in the spelling bee and, later, in the Year 10 Media exam did not fix Kellan's mindset, because she did not believe that her achievement was the result of natural ability. She knew that she had worked hard to get where she was. "I had a funny attitude to free time," she recalled of her early childhood. "Whereas other children would go out and play all the time, I just sat and read books." Neither of her parents had finished school; none of her extended family had ever been to university. Even in primary school, Kellan was teaching herself what she needed to know. This led to an early conviction that hard work could lead to success, and crucially she was in an environment – both at school and at home – where high achievement was recognised and celebrated. "At Chew [Valley]," she said, "there wasn't that negative peer pressure where kids got called 'nerds.' If anything, kids that got the higher grades got more respect. When I saw my grade and realised that I had done well, it was a great sense of achievement."

Kellan also described how public recognition of her work on school social media boosted her confidence as she realised that her hard work was paying off. "Nobody had ever done that before," she said of seeing her work publicly celebrated, "so I thought, 'if they think it's that good then maybe it really is.'" There was no risk of a Dweck-style intellectual paralysis after coming top of the class, because she recognised that it wasn't about who came first. "I was proud of myself," she said:

When other people did well, I was happy for them. I still knew that I was going to get a really good grade, and if they did too, then that was great. There was a bit of competition – we were all trying to outdo each other – but if they did well then I was going to do well too.

Kellan described her experience of sitting in the study centre when she moved on to her A-levels, seeing students all around her writing up notes and filling lever-arch files with work. "I thought maybe I'd better start doing that too," she recalled. Far from feeling threatened by the success of others, Kellan was inspired to work harder, to achieve more on her own terms.

In conversation with Kellan – a confident, self-possessed student, the first in her family to attend university – I was struck by the contrast between her approach to competition and my own at the same age. In my adolescent fixed mindset, I found competition oppressive as I measured my success against that of others; anything other than first made me a failure. Kellan, on the other hand, enjoyed the recognition and pride that success brought but, crucially, only measured that success against her own yardstick. "I think it's about 60 per cent talent and 40 per cent hard work," she said. "There was no way I was ever going to get above a C in Maths, but I knew I'd be disappointed with anything less than a B in English." She knew that she had worked hard and was doing well; she knew that if she continued to work hard, she would achieve the success that she deserved, irrespective of how anyone else did.

All must have prizes?

After the London 2012 Olympic Games, David Cameron laid out his vision for Britain in the pages of the *Daily Mail*, inspired by the weeks of competitions across the nation's capital. He wrote:

> in schools, there will be no more excuses for failure; no more soft exams and soft discipline. We saw that change in the exam results this year. When the grades went down a predictable cry went up: that we were hurting the prospects of these children. To that we must be very clear: what hurts them is dumbing down their education so that their potential is never reached and no one wants to employ them. "All must have prizes" is not just patronising, it is cruel – and with us it is over.[3]

I find this difficult, because I'm caught on the horns of a dilemma. On the one hand, I'm a fan of competition. I know that it can spur people on to achieve bigger and better things. I listened with interest to the documentaries commemorating the first four-minute mile, run by Roger Bannister on 5 May, 1954. Most commentators, and Bannister himself, agree that competition from Australian John Landy pushed him on to achieve that feat. And Kennedy's drive a decade later to put a man on the moon was driven more by competition with the Soviet Union than scientific advance. I'm also a fan of competitive sport, both as a spectacle and as an integral part of schooling within and beyond the curriculum. Despite all of this, I can't help feeling uneasy at the notion of awarding prizes to the single best performer in a discipline. When only one person can possibly come first, everything else seems like a failure. As my own experience of winning the English and Biology prizes showed, and as Carole Dweck's IQ-order sixth-grade seating plan reinforced, even though winning feels good, it can fix mindsets.

Learning from these experiences, I think there is only one competition that really matters – competition with oneself. If individual success is only measured relative to the success of others, then achievement is beyond the locus of control of the individual; you can't control how well someone else does, only how well you do. Achieving a personal best, rather than beating the opposition, should be the goal of each competitor. It is essential for all learners, child or adult, to have a clear and helpful understanding of how much better they are now than they were yesterday. It should not matter how well everybody else has done; the only question that matters is "have I improved?" Or perhaps to refine that model still further, "have I improved enough?" Placing your work in a hierarchy where you compare how well you have done with how well everybody else has done does not help you to improve. It may, perhaps, provide a competitive spur to some children, but it does not provide the mechanism or the means for improvement.

In fact, marks and grades which place students' work in a hierarchy create what Dylan Wiliam calls "ego-involving" feedback.[4] Such feedback places an emphasis on the learner and their self-esteem, encouraging a fixed mindset by creating a connection between the learner's own identity and the work they have produced. This is the kind of feedback that encourages a student to see themselves as the grade they have achieved, and which had led to generations of children seeing themselves as the levels they had attained at Key Stage 3: "I'm a 4c," "I'm a 3a," and so on. The seminal research that Wiliam and Paul Black carried out when looking at formative assessment shows that for feedback to be effective, it must be "task-involving" – that is to say, it must be focused on what the individual student needs to do to improve, not where they stand in relation to hierarchy or rank order. I will explore the idea of marking, assessment, and feedback in a growth mindset school in more detail in Chapter 10.

It is perhaps a sign of how slowly cultures change that even though Wiliam and Black have been patiently explaining this research since the late 1990s, almost two decades later, ego-involving feedback is still prevalent in our schools. It is clear to see the connections between ego-involving feedback and the fixed mindset. This ego-involving, mindset-fixing feedback can be given with the very best of intentions. The options for feedback to Dweck's young gymnast, Elizabeth, are all tempting – we want to make children feel good about their achievements. However, if we really want them to improve, we have to focus them on the process and strategies they need to use in order to make those improvements, and we have to instil in them the approach and self-discipline to make that stick.

I know now that it doesn't matter one jot whereabouts Kellan came in the rank-ordered spreadsheet of examination marks. What mattered to Kellan – and what I should have focused on more – was what she had done well and where she needed to improve to pick up the marks she'd missed. This is the message I teach in my classes now, the ethos I want for my school, and the frame of reference I set for myself.

Is growth mindset a fad?

My first external promotion – to the position of Second in English – took place just at the start of the National Strategies. Although by the end, the strategies had become a bloated behemoth, dragged into ineffectiveness under the weight of shiny lever-arch files, at the outset there was genuine enthusiasm and the chance to transform education. Structures for teaching writing, reading for understanding, and an attempt to codify teaching and learning so there was a consistent approach across the country were well intentioned and informed by research. But the imposition of a one-size-fits-all approach, however well intentioned, was problematic. Decontextualised lesson starters teaching aspects of grammar before a three-part-lesson (introduction, development, plenary) were mandatory for several years, leading to a generation of confused children, not really knowing what they were learning about or whether they were coming or going. The freedom to adapt your teaching approaches was removed. In doing so, teacher professionalism was undermined. Rather than taking a range of research-informed effective strategies and trusting the trained professional to select the best way to teach the material, the army of consultants and advisors claimed a monopoly on wisdom. It still amazes me how, at the time, the thousands of teachers went along with it all. But then, around the same time, I saw colleagues getting students to press their "brain buttons" to increase blood flow to their frontal lobe as part of the farcical Brain Gym craze.[5] I've used mandatory lesson plans in which I have had to identify how the activities I am planning cater for students with visual, auditory, or kinaesthetic learning styles, despite the fact that learning styles don't exist and therefore have no impact whatsoever on student learning or progress.[6] I've been there and seen the fads come and go.

Somehow, growth mindset seemed different. First, there wasn't a shiny lever-arch file and a paid-for subscription and set of resources. Dweck and her colleagues had produced significant impacts in studies they had conducted, and their methods were clearly presented as a template. But there wasn't a manual or a guru to follow, no one set way to implement the approach in your school. It was almost as if Dweck was saying, "here's the research. I think this is important and useful. Now it's up to you." This was encouraging and daunting in equal measure. We had the research to look to, but beyond that, implementing the strategy on a school-wide level would be a matter of deciding how to codify the research findings into systems, structures, and templates which were sufficiently specific to be rigorous, but sufficiently adaptable to be implemented across the rich variety of subject disciplines, age groups, learner dispositions, attitudes, and approaches that make up a secondary school. We would have to be thoughtful in our planning and rigorous in our evaluation. If something worked, we would need to try to replicate it. If something didn't work, we would need to be flexible, avoiding the sunk cost fallacy of persisting with it just because we had invested time, energy, and effort into its development.

Growth mindset schools

In thinking about launching growth mindset in schools, there are plenty of examples to look at. Many schools have dipped their toe in the water, or "done growth mindset," as part of their approach. However, there are fewer that have made mindsets a fundamental principle of their school ethos. One of the first schools in Britain to take this step, certainly that I have been able to find, is also one of the most striking.

New Heys School in Liverpool doesn't exist any more. The school was closed and merged with nearby St Benedict's Catholic College in September 2010 to form the Enterprise South Liverpool Academy. The building was demolished and a housing estate built on the site. But the story of the school's final years is as inspiring as it is remarkable. I first came across it in a paper delivered by James Kerfoot, Assistant Headteacher at New Heys from 2005 to 2010, on how they had implemented growth mindsets with some remarkable outcomes. I spoke to James about his experiences, and he had a fascinating story to tell.

James' appointment as Assistant Head at New Heys was his first senior leadership role. When he went for the interview, he was taken aback by the scale of the challenge. He found a school on the edge of chaos. Student behaviour was barely in control. Staff morale was low. Results were poor, plateauing at best and declining at worst. The role he had applied for was to take responsibility for teaching and learning, and professional development; he was daunted by the prospect and was on the verge of withdrawing, but the Head persuaded him to stay. Taking a deep breath, he agreed. He described how the senior team at New Heys faced a simple choice: they could try and police their way out of the crisis, containing student behaviour and asserting discipline to keep the institution running; or they could try and teach their way out of it. They chose the latter.

James implemented a new, compulsory system of staff development, overhauled appraisal, and focused everyone on the core business of improving teaching and learning. Progress was slow. Behaviour continued to be challenging. Staff morale stagnated. Then, in 2008, the school was notified of its impending closure. It wasn't hard to see the negative impact of such an announcement and the uncertainty and anxiety that it created. But at the same time, it was strangely liberating. The school had two years to try something different. They decided to see what would happen if they took the uncertainty that pervaded the school in the face of its own closure and made it a virtue. Using their status as a National School for Creativity, one of only fifty-six such schools in the country, they took on the challenge of becoming a growth mindset school to see what would happen. They called the project "The Uncertainty Principle."

Ten days in each school year were set aside for staff development, where the whole staff – not just teachers, but site and support staff – was trained in mindset approaches. The key aim of the project was "how to build up a toolkit to engender a growth mindset in yourself and your teams." James described one of the activities they undertook to try and get staff to think about the experience of learning – Wii Fit Skiing. Groups of staff in classrooms, the headteacher in with the caretaker, were taking on downhill slalom together with the aim of exploring what it feels like to fail publicly in front of your peers. And something amazing happened: where there had been grim-faced resignation, the bitterness and resentment that had pervaded the corridors was replaced with laughter and joy. Staff reflected on the experience of failure, on how it made them feel as they took on something they couldn't do. And they experienced progress as they learned from their mistakes and improved, coached and supported by one another. Sure, this was Wii Fit Skiing and not GCSE Chemistry. But the aim was to think about how they could use the experiences of the mindset training to create tools for themselves and their teams.

The focus of The Uncertainty Principle project was exclusively on developing staff. The aim was simple: the teachers needed to adopt a growth mindset for themselves and across their teams. As James said when I discussed it with him, the idea was to "work on the teachers – ignore the kids!" Coaching was implemented across the school, with each member of staff coaching and being coached. This was non-hierarchical, so the Head could be coached by the caretaker, a head of department by a less experienced teacher, a teaching assistant by an assistant head. It was all about helping one another to use the challenges of working together in this most challenging environment as opportunities to grow. Forty-eight developmental, ungraded peer observations took place in the first seven months of the 2009 school year, compared with only twelve over the entire 2007 school year. And this investment in staff development started to work.

The first impact that they noticed was an improvement in staff attendance. The headteacher has said, "staff wellbeing is paramount during this time, and the mindset training is key to our strategy for ensuring this." Absence reduced from an average of three and a half days per teacher per year to a little over one. Far from giving up and going through the motions, staff began to see that the challenges were not overwhelming and that there was still the chance to make a difference. As James himself said at the time: "the culture has become a really positive one in which the focus is clearly on learning, and problems are merely seen as barriers to be overcome." The testimonies of members of staff at New Heys bear out this assessment. "I have always thought that showing anyone that I was struggling was a sign of weakness; now I know that it is a sign I am a learner," said one. "I can honestly say that it has changed the way I view work and the way I operate in my classroom. It has helped me to see the positives in the school situation," said another. "The communication in the school is so much better after the training," said a third. "It is possible [now] to give feedback, and people are far less likely to become defensive." The growth mindset culture was taking root.

Another unexpected positive was the impact on staff retention. In a school faced with impending closure, it would perhaps be unsurprising if staff deserted in significant numbers: nobody wants to be left aboard a sinking ship. The school's prospects for recruiting strong replacements in such circumstances were bleak. However, in a culture where creative risk-taking in the classroom was celebrated and encouraged, where staff development was central to the school's mission, and where co-coaching was the prevalent model for that professional development, staff retention was high right up to the school's closure in 2010.

Perhaps most remarkably, however, and almost as an unintended consequence, something astonishing began to happen in the classrooms. Although the focus of the project had been exclusively on the development of a growth mindset in staff and their teams, teachers were beginning to model the approach in their classrooms. Students were starting to adopt the principles themselves. One Year 10 student said, "I have noticed lots of new ideas in my lessons. The teachers have really encouraged us to be okay with getting stuck and to find creative ways to get unstuck." A Year 8 student summed it up like this: "I am much happier to say 'I don't know,' and I don't feel stupid." And suddenly, unexpectedly, the results jumped. Between 2007 and 2009, the proportion of students achieving five or more GCSEs at grades A* to C increased by 39 per cent. Maths results improved by 17 per cent; English results by 28 per cent. The contextual value added figure, used by Ofsted in those days to assess school effectiveness, rose by 24 points. In the summer of 2010, New Heys School was shortlisted for the Outstanding Staff Training Initiative at the TES Innovation Awards. And then, in July, it closed.

James continues as a school leader today, working now as Head of his own school in Liverpool. He took the experiences of New Heys with him into headship, and he spoke enthusiastically about how he has developed the ideas over time. "It's so important," he said to me, "that we have a common language of 'stuckness' with our children." In his Headship, he has developed an approach to teaching and learning focused on the attributes needed for successful learning. Teachers need FACE: Feedback, Autonomy, Challenge, and Engagement; whereas students need KASH: Knowledge, Attitude, Skills, and Habits. These, in James' eyes, are the foundation stones of the growth mindset classroom, but they need a catalyst if they are going to work effectively. For James, that vital X-factor is trust. This is a theme to which I shall return in Chapter 6: trust between the students and their teachers, trust between the teachers and their colleagues, trust between leaders and the led – this is what makes successful learning possible. Without it, you have nothing.

Notes

1 Originally published in 2010.
2 Dweck, "Parents, teachers, and coaches."
3 Cameron, "Hard work, moral good and no more dumbing down."
4 Wiliam, "Enculturating learners into communities of practice."
5 See Ben Goldacre's annihilation of Brain Gym: "Banging your head repeatedly against the brick wall of teachers' stupidity."
6 Daniel Willingham patiently explains why learning styles don't exist: "Learning styles FAQ."

Bibliography

Cameron, D. (2012, 1 September). Hard work, moral good and no more dumbing down . . . It is time to stop the dithering that's holding Britain back. Retrieved 24 December, 2016, from *Mail Online*: www.dailymail.co.uk/news/article-2196870/DAVID-CAMERON-Hard-work-moral-good-dumbing—It-time-stop-dithering-thats-holding-Britain-back.html

Dweck, C. (n.d.). "Parents, teachers, and coaches." Retrieved 1 November, 2017, from *Mindset*: www.mindsetonline.com/howmindsetaffects/parentsteacherscoaches/

Goldacre, B. (2008, 16 February). Banging your head repeatedly against the brick wall of teachers' stupidity helps increase blood flow to your frontal lobes. Retrieved 19 April, 2017, from *Bad Science*: www.badscience.net/2008/02/banging-your-head-repeatedly-against-the-brick-wall-of-teachers-stupidity-helps-to-co-ordinate-your-left-and-right-cerebral-hemispheres/

Wiliam, D. (1998, September). Enculturating learners into communities of practice: Raising achievement through classroom assessment. Retrieved 24 December, 2016, from *Dylan Wiliam's Website*: www.dylanwiliam.org/Dylan_Wiliams_website/Papers.html

Willingham, D. (2012, 5 April). Learning styles FAQ. Retrieved 19 April, 2017, from *Daniel Willingham – Science and Education*: www.danielwillingham.com/learning-styles-faq.html

4 The Biscuit Club

Having read Dweck's work and chased down some of the research, it very quickly became apparent that this was an approach that I needed to adopt. The studies were clear about their implications for our practice. But how should we do it?

The first step was to run a pilot group. My colleague Ashley Loynton set about this task with a group of Year 11 boys, who became known as the Biscuit Club[1] because, as an incentive to participate, they were provided with plentiful chocolate biscuits in their lunchtime meetings. Ashley had been with me in Southampton for John Tomsett's talk, and we had eagerly been discussing the implementation of growth mindset back at school. He was keen to run the pilot group to test out some of the approaches suggested in the research and those from John Tomsett's school.

The boys were selected to take part in the pilot study for several reasons. The first reason was to look to address a disparity between boys' and girls' achievement in Science. Whilst achievement at C grade and above was on a par between boys and girls, a far greater proportion of girls was going on to achieve B, A, and A* grades. Our hypothesis was that some of the boys were "settling" for a C and not pushing themselves on towards the higher grades that they could achieve. Could a change in self-belief help? Could we create a programme for the boys that would create an intrinsic motivation which would help set them on course to realise their potential?

Second, the boys were facing the challenges of Year 11, with its exam pressures not just in Science but across the board. We hoped that a change in thinking could help support them across the curriculum, building their determination and providing them with the "grit" to keep at it over the course of the year. We hoped that we would see the benefits not just in Science, but in their approach across their subjects.

Finally, the boys themselves were keen and willing to be involved. Whether it was a heartfelt desire for self-improvement, the dawning realisation of the impending examination season, or the offer of free biscuits, we weren't sure, but the boys signed up voluntarily and agreed to work with us. In tribute to Ashley's enthusiastic Twitter habit, the boys insisted on adding a hashtag to the group's name: so #BiscuitClub was born.

The eleven boys concerned gave Ashley a manageable group to trial the programme we had devised and to get individual feedback on impacts, including changes to behaviour and attitude as well as outcomes.

The first step was to hold a brief introductory meeting to share with them the purpose of the group. This was about realising untapped potential and persuading the boys to set their sights beyond a C grade. We were very clear that a C grade would be a perfectly positive outcome, but that the purpose of the group was to get them to aim higher and strive for more. Ashley then explained that the group was a pilot for a strategy that we were hoping to roll out across the whole school. He promised that he would be transparent about the methods he was using, and that he would explain each intervention being used. He explained that this was different to the other in-school Year 11 intervention programmes we had, such as mentoring, adapted curriculum groups, one-to-one and small group tuition, or "booster" groups. The aim of this was not to "keep an eye on them" and make sure they were doing what they were supposed to, but rather to give them the tools to change their own behaviour and approach so that they could take responsibility themselves. However, as a trial, the boys would certainly not be responsible if the programme did not have the impact we had hoped, and there was no such thing as guaranteed success! All the boys agreed to the approach, and they met up shortly afterwards to begin the programme by completing an initial questionnaire.

Vitally, Ashley did not mention growth mindset ideas at any point in the initial meeting. The boys were joining #BiscuitClub to help them to raise their achievement, and that's all they knew. We wanted to be as sure as we could be that the students' completion of the questionnaires would not be susceptible to the Hawthorne effect, where data is skewed if, due to too much knowledge of the purpose of the assessment, respondents anticipate what sort of answers they ought to respond with. We wanted the boys to answer honestly, without trying to answer to "please the teacher" or second-guessing the answers they were "supposed" to give.

The questionnaire the boys completed consisted partly of a survey adapted from *Mindset*. Students were asked to respond to six statements using the scale:

- Strongly Agree (1)

- Agree (2)

- Mostly Agree (3)

- Mostly Disagree (4)

- Disagree (5)

- Strongly Disagree (6)

The statements were as follows:

1. You have a certain amount of intelligence, and you really can't do much to change it.

2. Your intelligence is something about you that you cannot change very much.

3. You can learn new things, but you can't really change your basic intelligence.

4. No matter who you are, you can change your intelligence a lot.

5. You can always greatly change how intelligent you are.

6. No matter how much intelligence you have, you can change it quite a bit.

Their responses to the first three questions were scored according to the scale listed above (although, of course, the boys didn't see the scores!) and averaged; this helped us to understand the mindset the boys were entering the project with. Scores of 3.0 or below suggested a fixed mindset, or a general belief that you cannot improve or change your intelligence. Scores of between 3.3 and 3.7 suggested a borderline profile, perhaps with some uncertainty about whether intelligence was fixed or not. Average scores of 4.0 and above suggested that students were entering the project with a growth mindset, or a belief that with effort and determination, intelligence can be improved. This gave us a rough baseline from which to see if the students' beliefs about intelligence could be changed over time as Dweck suggests they could be.

The second questionnaire contained a handful of open questions asking students to consider their interests in general. These were not school-specific questions. Vitally, this questionnaire also probed the boys' interpretations of success and their aspirations for the future. The questions were as follows:

- What are your interests and hobbies (if there are more than three, then feel free to list them)?

- What does success look like to you? What does it feel like? It may help to think of a time when you have been successful at something (anything, no matter how small or big).

- What would help you achieve even more success in school in general?

- What motivates you to do well at things you're interested in (like the things you mentioned as hobbies and interests)?

- Where would you like to be in 5 years? Doing what?

- Could Science play a role in your future subject choices or career choices? If yes, how?

- What could you be doing to ensure you end up successful in GCSE Science?

The main aims of the second questionnaire were to get the students to recognise the things they are interested in, and to discuss what motivated them to get better at those things, and whether there were lessons that could be learned from this to apply to school contexts. Many of the boys expressed an interest in their games consoles and described their ambitions to be the best player they could at *Call of Duty*. This was a jumping-off point to see if the boys could make the connection between the progress they made through hours of dedicated practice in front of the Xbox and the possibility that this approach could yield academic benefits if applied in school.

The second question was particularly important, and Ashley spent some time discussing the answers with the boys. The intention of asking the boys to try to relive success experiences emotionally was grounded in the work of Walter Mischel's *The Marshmallow Test*. As explained in Chapter 2, Mischel describes two separate impulse systems in the brain: the "hot" system and the "cool" system. The "hot" system is how Mischel refers to the limbic system, the primitive part of our brain concerned with basic drives and emotions such as fear, anger, hunger, and sex. The "hot" system is designed to act fast, predicated on a primal survival instinct. It does not concern itself with long-term consequences of actions, seeking only to resolve the immediate situation. The "cool" system, on the other hand, is crucial for future-oriented decisions and self-control. It is the system, centred primarily in the prefrontal cortex, that allows us to defer instant gratification for long-term gain by assessing situations, planning ahead, and considering cause-and-effect consequences. Fundamentally, it is the "cool" system which allows us to resist eating the first marshmallow by holding on to the future promise of the two-marshmallow reward.

Importantly, Mischel argues that the "cool" system does not fully mature until adulthood, in the early twenties, "leaving the young child as well as the adolescent greatly vulnerable to the vicissitudes of the hot system."[2] In order to counterbalance this, he suggests, it is important to use the "hot" system to help make long-term goals tangible and real. Telling a teenager that they need to work hard now if they want to have a good job in the future is often ineffective, because it appeals primarily to the "cool" system. It is suggesting a long-term reward – the good job in the future – for self-control in the present. But the problem is that many teenagers do not have a clear visualisation of the benefits of a good job in the future. Those that do probably already have well-activated cool systems, self-control, and dedication to study in order to achieve long-term goals. For the adults giving the advice, the benefits are immediate and clear: security, the ability to provide for your family, satisfaction in your work, holiday entitlement, and so on. But these are distant chimeras to most teenagers, who cannot conceive of these benefits.

Instead, in the questionnaire, Ashley tried invoke the students' "hot" systems to bring the benefits of self-control alive. By asking them to visualise success and to articulate what success felt like, he was attempting to create an emotional response which would bring the benefits of self-control in the here and now alive. In *The Marshmallow Test*, subjects imagined what the two marshmallows would taste like, their texture and their flavour, in order to make the benefits of waiting tangible and real. This was the same technique used to help the boys visualise their future selves being successful in Science and feeling again the positive emotions associated with previous success.

Over the half-term break after the initial meeting, Ashley collated the information from all eleven sets of questionnaires and compiled this alongside a breakdown of Fischer Family Trust (FFT) data that we held on each of the students. Of particular interest were the "chance charts," which showed the percentages of students nationally with similar prior attainment who had gone on to achieve different grades at GCSE Science.

Ordinarily our students would not see this data. At the time, they were given an aspirational target to aim for, called a "Challenge Grade," partially based on FFT data – a single grade for each subject. Our aim here was different, however. The purpose was not to tell them what they should achieve in terms of GCSE grades, but to emphasise that all outcomes were possible. For example, one student's data told him that 85 per cent of students nationally with the same prior attainment and socioeconomic background as him went on to get a C in Science. Forty-two per cent of those students went on to get a B, thirteen per cent of them an A, and five per cent of them an A*. The discussion that was held around this data was very powerful. They stood every chance of being in the 85 per cent. But what would they need to do to make themselves one of the 5 per cent? Because five out of every hundred students just like him had gone on to get an A* in Science. It was possible. And each student had the opportunity to exert some influence in making each of the outcomes from the chance chart more or less likely.

A second intervention based on the data involved discussing the fact that it had been created from a snapshot in time. One set of estimates was generated from the outcomes at the end of Key Stage 2 and a second set of estimates from the outcomes at the end of Key Stage 3. Far from being fixed, from the very moment the estimates were produced, they were subject to change. Our actions each and every day after that estimate is produced cause the probabilities of attaining a C, B, or A grade to change. Every element of progress made increases the probability of achieving the higher grades; every lapse or slip back decreases them. The key for students in the #BiscuitClub was to embrace the challenge of making the higher grades more achievable.

Table 4.1 Example "chance chart" from FFT Live (not from a member of the Biscuit Club!)

Name	DoB	Est Basis	Subject Group	% chance of achieving KS4 Grade								% chance		Grades		
				G+	F+	E+	D+	C+	B+	A+	A*	A*-C	Pass	GM	HGM	GA
		SE	Science	99.%	99.%	99.%	99.%	97.5%	81.5%	47.4%	13.7%	97.5%	99.%	B	47.4%	A
		SE	Science	99.%	99.%	99.%	99.%	98.8%	88.7%	59.6%	21.5%	98.8%	99.%	A	21.5%	S

The students' reactions to being confronted with data in this way were very powerful. They all knew their Challenge Grades, but seeing the possibilities of achieving the full range of grades presented to them in this way was a very positive experience. They realised – some of them for the first time – that other students just like them had gone on not just to succeed but to excel. This nameless 5 per cent of students with A* in Science became their competition. "If it was possible for them, it must be possible for me," came the response. Now, we needed to provide them with the tools to change and refine their approaches to increase the possibility of achieving the higher outcomes.

In order to facilitate this, Ashley gave the boys a short presentation which summarised mindset theory, explaining to them the key features of a growth mindset. We wanted to see whether simply being aware of the idea of a growth mindset was the powerful change agent that both he and I had experienced on reading about the research. The presentation also highlighted why a growth mindset might help them in achieving their own personal criteria for success and how it may help them stick at something which they found difficult. Here we went back to the Xbox examples the boys had cited to see if they could think about applying the same dedication to their studies as they did to the pastimes that personally interested them, even when the circumstances were challenging or difficult.

The boys also received their scores from the mindset assessment questionnaire they had taken in the earlier session. Ashley made them wait for this – and they kept on asking! However, it was important to understand the theory before being given their own questionnaire scores. They needed to understand that mindsets were mutable and changeable, and that for those of them with scores which placed them more towards the fixed mindset or entity learner end of the scale, this was an opportunity to change and develop their understanding.

Exploring the possibility of failure was also a key part of Ashley's presentation. It was important to counteract, from the outset, the mindset myth that adopting this approach would somehow instantaneously turn the Biscuit Club into world-beaters. Instead, he framed it for them like this: if you change your behaviours, approaches, and attitudes to learning, there is a chance that it will succeed in making a difference to the outcomes. The research would indicate that there is a good chance it will make a difference. However, if you do nothing, there is no chance that it will succeed.

Furthermore, the changes made had to be focused efforts on areas that would make a difference. We did not believe that simply trying harder was going to lead to success. That effort had to be channelled into those areas of the boys' approaches to school that would lead to the most improvement to their outcomes. Ashley used an example from his own proud Welsh heritage in rugby:

if you had one 6' 8" man weighing 18 stones and another 5' 8" man weighing 10 stones, one is better "adapted" to be an international second row rugby player, and the shorter, lighter chap may never succeed in this field (though he could maximise his own untapped potential). However, neither will the tall, heavy man become an international player if he never committed to training and invested time and effort to hard work, keeping going in the face of setbacks, injuries and inevitably losing a game. It is all about fulfilling your potential, whatever that may be, something all eleven boys could attempt to do in subjects in school in the next six months.[3]

Finally, Ashley took time to share answers about interests and aspirations, and to look at the boys' responses to the question "what does success look like?" These were powerful statements, targets which were much more motivating to them than the Challenge Grades that had been written into the front of their exercise books. In response to the question "what does success look like?" the boys had written:

> *Achieving your ambitions and having a job you enjoy.*
> *Gaining status or a respectable name for myself.*
> *Being the choice for someone in need of help.*
> *Making my family proud.*

What we saw in these responses was the activation of Mischel's "hot" system, but in the pursuit of long-term goals. The boys were articulating what it would feel like to them to be successful in education, in ways which were meaningful to them and which elicited the emotional response that a target grade could not. With the self-generated "hot system" targets in place, would the boys be motivated to take the necessary steps towards habit-changing in order to achieve them?

Over the following months, the Biscuit Club met regularly to review the strategies they were using towards achieving their goals. One of the most effective was using the language of "yet" to identify learning goals. The students took each area of the Science course in turn and filled in a learning reflection sheet to identify the areas of the course that they didn't know well enough . . . yet. This was then accompanied by one or two steps the boys could take to address the gap. The following week, the actions were reviewed, and the boys reflected again on how successful they had been in securing their own understanding. The powerful change here was that the boys themselves were driving the process – identifying their own areas for development, deciding the actions and strategies they were going to use to address them, and honestly evaluating their impact in the following week. By taking ownership of their own progress, they were beginning to enact the essential learning behaviours that would lead to improvements in their outcomes.

The highlight of the Biscuit Club project came from Twitter. Ashley had issued the participants with copies of Nigel Holmes' infographic illustrating the fixed and growth mindsets.[4] The handout was designed to act as a visual reminder of the attitudes and behaviours the boys needed to be demonstrating in order to change their mindsets. On the evening of bonfire night, Jack, one of the Biscuit Club students, tweeted a picture of the mindset infographic secured with masking tape over the power button on his Xbox and adorned with the legend "Read this before switching on #Ashuallycaring."[5] This was the first concrete sign that the messages of the mindset intervention were starting to sink in. Jack had taken a positive step to change his habits and behaviour. Now, in order to switch his Xbox on when he got home, he would actually have to lift the mindset infographic out of the way first, making an active choice to ignore the strategies that he had put in place for himself – namely, completing his revision when he got home and using his console as a reward for achieving his goals. That, and the solid-gold pun in the hashtag, gave us the courage of our convictions.

Did it actually make a difference? Well, the boys had finished Year 10 with two B grades, eight Cs, and a D in Science between them. In their December mock exams, they had achieved one A*, one A, five Bs, three Cs, and a D. It was clearly making a difference to some of them! But, reflecting on it afterwards, Ashley said, "the greatest reward as a teacher has been their change in attitude; a greater 'can do' or, at least, 'I will try' approach." It was enough to convince us that our plan to implement the approach across the whole school had merit.

Ashley agreed to present his findings from #BiscuitClub to the whole school as part of the launch event the following March, on our whole-school Inset day. He summarised his advice as follows:

- Imparting knowledge about a growth mindset is one possible key step to getting students to change how they approach their learning, or at least start this change process.

- You must always maintain high expectations of students for growth mindset ideas to bear fruit.

- A shift in your use of language is essential, from "I can't do that" to "I can't do that . . . YET."

- In giving feedback on pieces of work, the focus must be on the process of effort and hard work and what was done to achieve the outcome or, equally important, what could be done to improve the outcome.

- Be sincere with your classes and share with them your experiences of failure, share with them how you overcame it, and model learning to them.

It's great to look back on #BiscuitClub as the initial testing ground for the ideas and practices that would become so embedded in my own practice and our school culture over the coming years. The experience of those eleven boys formed a crucial part of the launch to staff at Chew Valley in March, lending credibility and practical application to the theory. Whenever I explain our approach to a group of staff, I always come back to the image of the infographic taped over the Xbox power switch and the fact that our students – or one of them at least – was #AshuallyCaring.

Notes

1 Loynton, "Set your mind to it." With grateful thanks to Ashley Loynton for permission to adapt his blog post about the Biscuit Club for this chapter.
2 Mischel, *The Marshmallow Test*, page 46.
3 Loynton, op. cit.
4 Holmes, "Gallery."
5 You can see the image from this original tweet in Ashley's blog, op. cit.

Bibliography

Berger, R. (2003). *An Ethic of Excellence.* Portsmouth, NH: Heinemann.
Duckworth, A. (2016). *Grit.* London: Vermilion.
Dweck, C. (2012). *Mindset: How You Can Fulfil Your Potential.* London: Robinson.
Holmes, N. (2016, September). Gallery. Retrieved 1 December, 2016, from Nigel Holmes' website: www.nigelholmes.com/site/wp-content/uploads/2016/09/two_mindsets.png
Loynton, A. (2013, 24 November). Set your mind to it. Retrieved 30 November, 2016, from *Teaching and Nerding*: https://ashleyloynton.wordpress.com/2013/11/24/set-your-mind-to-it-exploring-growth-mindset-ideas/
Mischel, W. (2015). *The Marshmallow Test.* London: Transworld Publishers.
Syed, M. (2011). *Bounce.* London: Fourth Estate.
Tomsett, J. (2015). *This Much I Know about Love Over Fear.* Carmarthen: Crown House Publishing.
Willingham, D. T. (2009). *Why Don't Students Like School?* San Francisco: Jossey-Bass.

5 Launching growth mindset with staff

I first launched the idea of becoming a growth mindset school in March 2014 at Chew Valley School. I still maintain that this was the single most successful Inset day I've run. The concept gave the school a clear vision to align behind and carried us forward with a sense of direction and momentum into the coming years. It was the success of this day, and the sense of unity of purpose that it provided, which shaped my own vision of education into the future and made it such a hallmark of my own school leadership. Since that day in 2014, I have taken the concept forward into my own Headship, and I have also worked with other schools to help them shape their own journey into understanding and applying the vision and values of a growth mindset in their particular contexts. In this chapter, I will outline that first growth mindset programme from 2014 and explain how it has been refined and developed in future iterations.

When introducing any initiative or concept, it is essential to ensure that the professionals in the audience take ownership of its delivery. When launching growth mindset for the first time, I had some ideas about how it might be implemented across the school – but I didn't have it all worked out. The aim for the day was to introduce Dweck's research, the rationale for its application, and the principles of mindset theory. Then it was over to the staff to think about how this might be applied in a school context. Although, in the first instance, this was my own school context, providing this ownership of the application of the principles has been an essential part of any work I have done on growth mindset. There isn't a single right way to do it. It's really up to you.

In planning the day, I tried to follow the pattern of Dweck's own book. Essentially, this breaks down into three stages:

1. Understand the concept of fixed and growth mindsets

2. Introduce the neuroscience that underpins mindset theory

3. Explore the influences we can exert to shift mindsets

As a starter, it's always interesting to ask staff to fill out a questionnaire to see where they currently are on the scale of fixed mindset to growth mindset. I've never collected this data in! But it does help to highlight our own beliefs about intelligence, and it makes for a good talking point on tables. Of course, if your training day programme has been published in advance with the title "Chris Hildrew introduces the concept of growth and fixed mindsets, and the influence of beliefs about intelligence and ability on success," it's likely that responses to the questionnaire are going to be influenced by the Hawthorne effect in any case!

It's also important to present a rationale for the change. Why is growth mindset important? Of course, there is the substantial research evidence to support the efficacy of mindset interventions on student progress, attainment, and well-being. This is persuasive in and of itself. But for me, fundamentally, it is the antidote to the toxin of the teacher being the hardest-working person in the room. A mindset shift requires an emphasis on the attitude and behaviour of the learners in the classroom, where the effort expended by the learner is correlated to the progress and outcomes they achieve. This is not usually a difficult sell to an audience of hard-working teachers: shift the emphasis from the teacher to the students. Ensure that the actions you take in the classroom are directly linked to an impact on the effort, strategies, and approaches taken by the learners. Make them work hard – it's the key to them making the progress and learning gains we all want to see.

As an aside, I must emphasise that in this chapter, by "staff" I mean all staff from across the school. Too often I have seen an unnecessary divide between teaching and support staff in relation to professional development and training. Of course, there will be some specific aspects of training that are more relevant to classroom-based staff, but this is not one of them. The redevelopment of the ethos and approach of a school is one that involves all the staff, all the students, and all the families that are part of the school's community. If you are going to redesign reports, for example, it would be possible for the administrators to "just do as they're told" and implement the changes recommended by senior teachers. But how much more effective is it when those administrators understand the principles that are being implemented? How much more effective will the systems be when those who run their administration are involved in their design?

The NASA principle

If you are going to ensure that all of the school's community is aligned around a growth mindset ethos – from the headteacher to the classroom teacher, from the teaching assistant to the lunchtime supervisor, from the site staff to the receptionist – it is essential that every adult models the approach and applies it to their own work, learning to continuously improve and develop whichever aspect of the school's provision they are responsible for. This is what my ex-colleague Chris George refers to as the NASA principle.

Before he retired, Chris and I spent a fantastic hour in my office, during which he generously shared with me the wisdom he had accrued over his long career in teaching. One of those gems was to always take a piece of paper with you when you move around the school site. There doesn't have to be anything written on it – any piece of paper will do. If people see you in the corridor carrying a piece of paper, they will assume you are on an important mission to get that piece of paper to wherever it needs to be as soon as possible, and they will leave you in peace. Empty-handed, you are fair game for whatever particular problem needs sorting! I have tried this technique myself, and I can report 100 per cent reliability in my semi-scientific action research on the topic.

Aside from this exceptionally useful advice, Chris also told me the story of President John F. Kennedy's visit to NASA Space Center in 1962. Following his famous speech at Rice Stadium, Kennedy was checking on the progress of the nation's efforts to put a man on the moon before the end of the decade. During the visit, he noticed a janitor carrying a broom. He stopped the official tour and approached the janitor. "Hi," the President said, "I'm Jack Kennedy. What are you doing?" The janitor looked back at the President and said, "Well Mr President, I'm helping to put a man on the moon." The janitor understood that his work at NASA was part of the larger effort focused on the single purpose, the vision that would eventually be realised by Apollo 11.

Chris' story of the NASA principle reminded me of a story that I had already heard, and which I always use when discussing leadership: the story of the three stonemasons. The story goes that a man happened across three stonemasons working hard on a construction site, chipping away at huge blocks of stone to fashion them into blocks of the correct size and shape. The first seemed unhappy at his job, hammering at his chisel but frequently stopping to check the time. When the man asked what it was that he was doing, the first mason responded, rather curtly, "I'm hammering this stupid rock, and I can't wait 'til 5 when I can go home."

A second mason, seemingly more interested in his work, was hammering diligently. When asked what it was that he was doing, he answered, "Well, I'm moulding this block of stone so that it can be used with others to construct a wall. It's not bad work, but I'll sure be glad when it's done."

The third mason was hammering at his block with real energy, taking time to stand back and admire his work. He chipped off small pieces until he was satisfied that it was the absolute best he could do. When the bystander asked him about his work, he stopped, gazed skyward, and proudly proclaimed, "I am building a cathedral!"

Seeing to it that every member of staff understands their contribution to the wider project ensures all are engaged in purposeful, meaningful work. The network technician who changes the bulb in the data projector is contributing their part to the clarity of communication that ensures that the lessons are learned. The administrator who provides the child's assessment data and education plan to the teacher is helping to ensure that the learning that day is accessible, pitched at the right level, and effective. These are the cement that holds the blocks of the learning together. The tutor who registers that child in the morning and makes sure they are safe and happy, reminding them of the learning targets that they had sent home to their family last week and sending them off to period one in the right frame of mind, lays the foundation stones for the wall. Each teacher explaining an individual concept or idea in a single lesson on a Wednesday afternoon is an integral part of the cathedral of that child's education. Were any single part of the edifice to be prepared incorrectly, there is a risk that the towers will lean and the windows will fall out.

Everyone who works in a school needs to understand their contribution to the wider vision and purpose. When re-evaluating and reconstituting the vision, therefore, all who work there need to be involved, to have their say, and to take that vision forward into their own individual role.

Understanding the concept of fixed and growth mindsets

There is a wealth of material available to explain mindset theory. In my first growth mindset day in 2014, I used Eduardo Briceño's TEDx Manhattan Beach talk from 2012: "The power of belief: mindset and success."[1] This talk had been influential in helping me to understand the ideas behind mindset theory, and he makes a persuasive case for the adoption of growth mindset approaches in schools in his conclusion. Since then, Dweck herself has recorded a TED talk proper – *The power of believing you can improve*[2] – and the RSA has produced one of its fantastic animations to accompany her talk – *How to help every child fulfil their potential*.[3] This video is now my go-to source for introducing the concept. In a little under ten minutes, Dweck outlines the key studies from her research into the impact of mindsets on achievement, and on the use of praise to transmit mindsets. It's an accessible precis, and, I find, it helps to hear it direct from Dweck herself.

Following on from the video introduction, a few key points are worth highlighting. These are the three "mindset rules" which govern behaviour in the two mindsets. First, how you want to appear to others. In a fixed mindset, your goal is to look clever at all costs. In a growth mindset, your goal is to learn at all costs. Second, how you respond to setbacks. In a fixed mindset, a setback is a judgment on you as a person: you become a failure. In a growth mindset, a setback allows you to confront mistakes and deficiencies: you experience failure and learn from it. Finally, what you believe about talent and effort. In a fixed mindset, you believe that if you are talented, you shouldn't have to try hard; it should come naturally. In a growth mindset, you believe that it is effort which activates your ability and leads to success.

For most of us, it is natural to sit somewhere in between the two extremes. It is very rare indeed to find someone who scores a perfect 100 per cent on any growth mindset questionnaire – even with the Hawthorne effect as a following wind! It's also useful to explore the idea that mindsets can be domain-specific at this stage.

For example, there are many people who will happily spend hours practising their golf swing or tennis serve, looking for fractional improvements in distance or speed, but will then say, "I can't cook" or "I'm useless at maths." With teachers, I usually find that there is an implicit understanding that nudges us towards a belief in growth, even before the introduction of mindset theory. But whether we practise this belief in our own work and life is another matter, and whether we consider the transmission of mindsets to children in our classes is still more complex.

Introducing the neuroscience that underpins mindset theory

There are several great options to introduce neuroscience to teachers. The first – and most successful in my book! – is to find a willing Psychology teacher who knows about the subject to prepare a short section on what happens in the brain when we learn something new. In the absence of a volunteer, the Khan Academy is an excellent resource for material on many topics and this one in particular.

Sal Khan founded his website of educational videos in 2005 to help his cousins with their homework.[4] It now reaches more than ten million users around the world with over five thousand courses.[5] Fundamental to the vision of the online Academy is the belief that "you can learn anything," and the site contains an invitation to "start learning on the Khan Academy: build your growth mindset"[6] alongside a video conversation between Khan and Dweck. As the Khan Academy is a non-profit built on the principle that it is "For Free. For Everyone. Forever," it is a superb resource for teachers and students across the globe.

As part of the "you can learn anything" campaign, the Khan Academy has released a ten-minute tutorial called *Human brain and growing intelligence*[7] and a shorter summary version called *How to grow your brain*.[8] Both these videos explain the basics of neural plasticity through the idea that the brain is like a muscle. When we work out a muscle in a gym, we make it struggle. To compensate for this struggle, our bodies grow the muscle and strengthen it. With repeated struggle, our muscles grow stronger, more efficient, and more effective. The same thing happens in our brains as we struggle: "the more we use it, the stronger it gets." The brain actually grows new and stronger connections between the billions of neurons, or brain cells, as we learn new things. Importantly, the connections grow stronger from the experience of struggle and reviewing errors than they do from the practice of already mastered skills. The notion of a growth mindset is not just a theory, but a demonstrable process, showing what happens in our brains when we learn something new.

Exploring the influences we can exert to shift mindsets

When teachers complete a mindset questionnaire, this is a helpful point to review the scores. How many of them describe themselves as the score they achieved?

How many of them say, "I am a 4.5" instead of "I got a 4.5"? There is a risk that we can become fixed-mindset about our own mindsets! Vital to the understanding of the work of Dweck, Duckworth, and others is the fact that we can change our own beliefs about learning. If we understand more about the neuroscience, more about the impact of beliefs about learning, and more about how changing those beliefs can influence our outcomes, we can be motivated to shift our mindsets away from fixed and towards growth. This can happen across the board or one domain at a time. Crucially, it is up to each individual. Whilst you can present the evidence and make an overwhelming case in favour of mindset theory, what you cannot do is actually change someone's mind for them. That is something that only they can do themselves.

As teachers, therefore, it is important for us to consider what we can change in order to exert an influence on the beliefs that children hold about their own ability and intelligence. What can we do to help them change their own minds? What would we need to do differently, in our own school, to encourage a growth mindset in our staff and students? What would we need to do to make it the only logical way to learn? What would it look like, feel like, and sound like if we worked in a growth mindset school?

These were the questions I posed towards the end of my presentation at Chew Valley in March 2014, and they are the questions which I always pose whenever I am introducing the concept to a group of teachers. This encourages staff to think through the systems, approaches, and culture of the institutions in which they work and to evaluate them for the ways in which they transmit mindsets to those who work there. The process of staff critiquing and reimagining the systems of the school to align more closely to a growth mindset creates the ownership I described earlier, but it also ensures that the redevelopment of the approaches within the school is shared, and reliant not just on one senior leader but on the wisdom and experience of everyone present. In further iterations of my work on growth mindsets in schools, I have broken down the question into headings, asking how a growth mindset school would approach:

- Leadership (including student leadership)

- Pastoral care and systems

- The curriculum

- Target setting

- Assessment

- Reporting

- Feedback

- Lesson planning and delivery

- Professional development

- The community

It is often helpful to ask tables of staff to address each aspect for ten minutes or so, capturing their thoughts on large sheets of paper, then passing their paper on to the next table for another ten minutes. In the second round, staff can review the ideas generated by the first group and add to, critique, or develop those ideas before passing them on again. I usually find that three or four rotations, perhaps with diminishing time allowances, gives enough opportunity to fill the sheets with ideas. Posting the sheets along a wall in a gallery and allowing browsing time then also provides a good opportunity for staff to get up and stretch their legs, looking along the wall at the ideas they have generated along with those generated by other groups, seeing the connections, and looking at the ways in which each aspect of the school interacts, meshes, and relates with the others. Reimagining a school in this way, centred on a single binding principle, is a powerful and unifying approach to improvement, which provides both purpose and direction.

Each school is unique. The systems currently in place will be different. The approach, ethos, and culture will have developed over time in response to the circumstances, challenges, and demands of the school's particular context. However, any change will require an evaluation of the status quo and an examination of the effectiveness of existing systems in the light of the most up-to-date evidence available. As Grace Hopper says, "the most dangerous phrase in the language is: 'we've always done it this way.'"[9] Considering how systems, processes and approaches might be reimagined allows you to identify those areas of practice that have become routine not because of their impact or effectiveness, but simply because of their familiarity. Some changes might not be radical or fundamental; they may only require a shift of emphasis. Others may be more significant and may require the slaughter of sacred cows. The unification of purpose and approach that becoming a growth mindset school provides is a basis for alignment of any change and for evaluation against that mission and value set.

Over the coming chapters I will explain how a growth mindset ethos has shaped the systems in the schools in which I have worked. These won't necessarily work in every school; they may not work in your school. It will be far more effective if you and your colleagues do as we did and examine and re-evaluate the systems and approaches you currently use and redesign them for yourselves.

Notes

1 Briceño, "The power of belief."
2 Dweck, "The power of believing you can improve."
3 Dweck, "How to help every child fulfil their potential."
4 Khan, "Meet the team."
5 Dreifus, "It all started with a 12 year old cousin."

6 Khan, "You can learn anything."
7 Khan, "Human brain and growing intelligence."
8 Khan, "How to grow your brain."
9 Hopper, computer scientist and US Navy Rear Admiral, is quoted in Grosch, *Library Information Technology and Networks*, page 183.

Bibliography

Briceño, E. (2012, 18 November). The power of belief: Mindset and success. Retrieved 23 December, 2016, from *YouTube*: https://youtu.be/pN34FNbOKXc

Dreifus, C. (2014, 27 January). It all started with a 12 year old cousin. Retrieved 23 December, 2016, from *The New York Times*: https://www.nytimes.com/2014/01/28/science/salman-khan-turned-family-tutoring-into-khan-academy.html?_r=0

Dweck, C. (2014, 17 December). The power of believing you can improve. Retrieved 23 December, 2016, from *YouTube*: https://youtu.be/_X0mgOOSpLU

Dweck, C. (2015, 15 December). How to help every child fulfil their potential. Retrieved 23 December, 2016, from *The RSA*: https://www.thersa.org/discover/videos/rsa-animate/2015/how-to-help-every-child-fulfil-their-potential

Grosch, A.N. (1995). *Library Information Technology and Networks*. New York: Marcel Dekker.

Khan, S. (2014, 7 August). Human brain and growing intelligence. Retrieved 23 December, 2016, from *YouTube*: https://youtu.be/wCBlTX3quzs

Khan, S. (2014, 14 August). How to grow your brain. Retrieved 23 December, 2016, from *YouTube*: https://youtu.be/GWSZ1DKjNzY

Khan, S. (2016). Meet the team. Retrieved 23 December, 2016, from *Khan Academy*: https://www.khanacademy.org/about/the-team

Khan, S. (2016). You can learn anything. Retrieved 23 December, 2016, from *Khan Academy*: https://www.khanacademy.org/youcanlearnanything

6 Leading with a growth mindset

In 2012, I started a blog. I had been inspired by headteacher bloggers such as Tom Sherrington[1] and John Tomsett,[2] who share their experiences of school leadership generously, freely, and with wisdom and humanity. I was also, at the time, completely incensed by the proposal from the then Secretary of State at the Department for Education, Michael Gove, to do away with GCSEs and replace them in English Baccalaureate subjects with English Baccalaureate Certificates, only accessible to the higher-attaining students in the country. That proposal was never enacted, which somewhat restored my faith in the power of government consultations; clearly I also have Michael Gove to thank for the impetus behind my first foray into blogging.

The title of my blog is *Teaching: Leading Learning*,[3] reflecting my long-held belief that the skills of classroom teaching and leadership are intrinsically intertwined and that the very act of teaching is an act of leadership. In both cases, you are in charge of a group of people and you want to take them from one situation or state, to another. You have to enact change. There are several ways you can accomplish this, which might be linked to teaching styles or to leadership styles. For example, an authoritarian teacher might say: "I am the teacher. I am in charge. This is what we're doing now, whether you like it or not"; an authoritarian leader might say: "I am the boss. I am in charge. This is what we're doing now, whether you like it or not."

A second style I dub the "apologist." In a classroom situation, this might manifest as: "I know this is boring. I don't really like it either. But it's on the exam specification so we have to do it; let's just make the best of it." A school leader enacting the apologist style might say: "I know this is ridiculous. I don't really like it either. But the Department for Education has said we have to have performance-related pay so let's try to make the best of it."

The third style, my preferred approach, is values-driven teaching and leadership. The values-driven classroom teacher might stand in front of the class and say: "This is brilliant. This is why I got into teaching in the first place. Let's have a look at it together." The values-driven leader would stand in front of the staff saying: "This is brilliant. This will improve all of us, make us more effective, and help the children. Let's have a look at it together." This values-driven style is the one where I teach at my best. It happens when I am teaching a book or poem that I love, maybe for its quality, its cultural capital and value, or the way in which it speaks to us on a fundamental level about our own human condition. By happenstance, it may be that this book or poem is part of a GCSE or A-level specification or course, but more usually I will have chosen it myself to illustrate a particular idea or to demonstrate a particular concept. That element of choice means that I am using my own drive to teach to bring the lesson to bear. It happens when I can see the bigger picture of what I am teaching and how this lesson is one crafted block in the cathedral of the child's education. It happens when I know that I am making a difference in that lesson.

In leadership, it happened when I launched growth mindset to staff. A growth mindset approach had not been imposed on me or my school by an external agency, meaning that I had not been forced into an apologist style. The implementation of the approach was designed to be shared, meaning that an authoritarian style was neither necessary nor desirable. Instead, I was presenting a way of thinking and approaching learning which was adaptable and flexible, that was grounded in substantial research, and which I truly believed would make a difference to the staff and students in the school. I was at my most confident because the content was owned and shaped by us, in our context, with every member of staff and student able to contribute to its construction. For me, the ideas of a growth mindset school align completely with the values I hold about education, learning, and leadership. Above all, as a school leader, I need to model the growth mindset in the schools I lead.

It is leaders who ensure that the vision and mission statements become a lived reality in the day-to-day work of the school. The unity of purpose around becoming a growth mindset school must be felt and lived by all its leaders – from the headteacher to the student council, the classroom teacher to the site manager. For that reason, the growth mindset leader must lead *with* a growth mindset and lead *for* a growth mindset.

Fixed mindset leadership pitfalls

Dweck devotes an entire chapter of *Mindset* to leadership. In it, she cites the now well-worn example of the collapse of Enron under Jeff Skilling and Kenneth Lay, which was also the subject of analysis in Malcolm Gladwell's "The Talent Myth."[4] She also describes the rise and subsequent fall of Chrysler under Lee Iacocca, amongst others. In her business-focused chapter, she describes how fixed mindset leadership undermines the ability of organisations to sustain success. There are several pitfalls to avoid.

The first trap is ego. Dweck cites the Chrysler CEO Lee Iacocca as an example of the fixed mindset "hero leader" who uses leadership as a validation of their own brilliance, interested more in their own reputation and legacy than in that of others. The "hero leader" is more focused on the actions within the organisation which will look good, which will create the right impression, which will make them seem superior. Above all, it is about the leader themself, rather than the organisation.

I have met leaders like this in education. I know some even now. I worry that the burgeoning CEO culture as multi-academy trusts grow and develop around the country is encouraging a new breed of educational silverbacks, beating their chests and proclaiming themselves the kings of the jungle. There are already stories circulating of CEOs using educational funding to pay for large expense accounts, corporate hospitality, and the trappings of commercial success. This kind of ego-involved leadership is bred from the competitive world. A culture which sees educational establishments – whether that be teachers, departments, schools, or multi-academy trusts – as competitive is futile. After all, who "wins" or "loses" if one is better than another? In the end, it is the students. The kind of leadership which seeks to find a competitive edge over rivals is the kind that seeks out low-value qualifications to boost league table positions, paying scant regard to the quality of education provided to the young people and favouring instead cheap value-added points. It is this culture which can lead to schools, teachers, and departments "hoarding" successful strategies and refusing to share them for fear that if others got hold of them, they would lose their competitive edge. I have seen this happening. Those that lead with this approach have surely lost sight of the fact that the children in the other school are just as deserving as those in their own; they have lost sight of the responsibility of all of us to be "system leaders" and to educate for all children, not just those we have in front of us today.

The second trap also takes its name from Gladwell's 2002 article on the Enron scandal: "The Talent Myth." This trap has at its centre the belief that innate ability (or talent) outweighs all else. For Dweck, it encapsulates fixed mindset thinking. That is not to say that talent has no place in schools, but simply that talent alone is not enough. Talent without a growth mindset, like the hare in the race with the tortoise, is set to lose. Or, as basketball star Kevin Durant says: "hard work beats talent when talent fails to work hard." Recruiting the most talented individuals you can find to your school is vital, but more important than their talent is their attitude and beliefs, their values, and their approach to the task. A belief in the superiority of talent, as we have seen, can lead to a culture where mistakes are hidden, deficiencies are ignored, and anything which might jeopardise the perception that this is "the smartest guy in the room" is rejected. At the same time it can also lead to unscrupulous practices to retain the most talented staff, offering retention allowances or "jobs for the boys" promotions. This is short-termism in action; leading and developing staff includes recognising the inevitability that, eventually, the investment you have made in them will lead them to leave your school and work in another – and this is okay. The students in their next school will benefit, and your students, in their turn, will benefit from the recruitment of a colleague with all the development invested in them by their previous school. Focusing on talent alone is the opposite of growth mindset leadership.

The team pursuit model of leadership

At the London 2012 Olympics, I became completely obsessed with the track cycling event. I know I am not alone in this, since most of the nation seemed glued to their screens as the British Cycling medal factory accrued seven golds and one silver at the velodrome. Much has been made of the team's philosophy of the aggregation of marginal gains, and their approach has much of the growth mindset about it. The event which most captured my imagination was the team pursuit. In this event, a team of four riders (three for the women in 2012, although parity was reached by the next games in Rio) set off and hurtle round the track like a train, chasing their opposition who start on the other side of the circuit. The role of the train's "engine," the rider at the front powering along and shielding the others in their slipstream, rotates so that all members of the team share the workload. The following riders bring their front wheels to within millimetres of the rider in front to maximise aerodynamic efficiency, matching their speed and rhythm as one; all members of the team are working in complete harmony towards the same goal, with and for each other. On the sidelines, the coach stands. As the team thunders past, the coach takes one step to the left or right of the start/finish line to indicate whether the team is ahead of or behind the pace they have set for themselves.

Although the discipline is called a "pursuit" and, nominally, you are chasing the opposition team around the track, it's very rare indeed for one team actually to catch the other over the course of a 4,000-metre race. What you are actually working against is the clock, trying to post the best time. The target – the opposition team – is always out of reach, disappearing round the bend before you see them. And they get the same view of you, because just as you are trying to catch up with them, they are trying to catch up with you, and you are disappearing round the bend at the top of the track just as they are disappearing round the bend at the bottom. Both teams benefit from having something to chase, a benchmark or standard to aim for, but it is your own time you are trying to beat. I remember watching in 2012 as Dani King, Laura Trott, and Joanna Rowsell set a new world record in qualifying, then beat it in the semi-final, then beat it again in the final. They were so far ahead of the opposition that their only real competition was themselves.

The other great thing about the team pursuit is that the time for the team is taken from the last rider over the line. The team is only as good as its slowest member. There are no "heroes" in team pursuit: every member of the team has to do their best if they are to succeed. The discipline cannot rely on individual superstars.

So, where is the leadership in the track cycling team pursuit? In one sense, the coach is the leader. This is the person who has directed the team, honed their performance, given them feedback over months and months of training to help them improve. They don't get a lot of coverage on TV. They're really quite self-effacing, just implementing tiny nudges on the start/finish line to ensure that the cyclists, travelling at over 60 kilometers per hour, stay on course. On the other hand, there's a leader on the track every other lap. Everybody takes their turn, and the contribution of every rider counts towards the final result. When you're out in front, it's your job to keep the pace high, but you have to take the rest of the team with you – you can't go off too quickly, because if a gap opens up between you and the rider behind, you lose the aerodynamic efficiency. And, whilst you're up there at the front, you're shielding the riders behind, looking after them by minimising the drag on their bike.

Team pursuit encapsulates the core principles of leadership for me. A shared goal binds the team together, a mutual commitment to excellence which drives the whole forward. Yet the responsibility for chasing that goal is shared evenly between every member of the team. Each individual takes a leadership responsibility at a different stage of the race. When you are a leader, you set the pace, set the direction, and keep the momentum going while, at the same time, shielding those who follow you and ensuring that they have to expend the least amount of energy possible to get the job done. The coach – I suppose the closest thing to a headteacher that team pursuit has – is not the one hammering round the track. The coach directs from the edge, providing feedback and encouragement to keep things going, having built the systems to support that culture over the months and years beforehand. The team's performance is counted from the slowest rider, meaning that nobody is left behind. This is what leadership means to me.

To lead with a growth mindset, the notion of competition between teachers, departments, schools, or trusts must first be set aside in favour of the belief that we are all one team. Fundamental to the success of education is the principle that we only succeed if we all succeed. This means that it is the goal of leadership to ensure that everyone who works in the institution – students, teachers, non-teaching staff – is lined up on the wheel of the person in front, knowing exactly what they are doing, working at the fine margins to eke out the last possible fraction of high performance. Every teacher in every lesson takes their turn at the front, setting the pace and minimising the drag to ensure maximum progress is made, before sending the students off to the next lesson in the right frame of mind, with the right attitude, keeping the momentum. The leader should be there on the sideline, providing feedback by stepping slightly to the left or the right, setting the tempo, and keeping the focus where it needs to be. But when the medals are handed out, it's the cyclists who step up to the podium and deserve the applause and adulation.

The culture we set in our schools should be one of continual improvement, training each aspect of our performance to perfection, whether we are staff or students, in order to achieve excellence.

The seats on the bus or love the one you're with

Jim Collins' *Good to Great* is usually cited as the definitive guide to leadership, quoted and referenced and set as required reading. Certainly Dweck makes significant use of Collins' thesis in *Mindset*, and the leadership characteristics he identifies in his study of successful leaders in business bear all the hallmarks of a growth mindset. These leaders are self-effacing, they learn from failure and difficulty, they only compete with themselves, and they have an unshakeable belief in the continuous improvement of themselves and their organisations that will lead them to thrive in the long term. These are all qualities that educational leaders should aspire to, and they are certainly characteristics of the growth mindset.

Collins' book also contains what I see as an unhelpful leadership metaphor: the seats on the bus. In this section of *Good to Great*, Collins likens the organisation to a bus, and the leader to a bus driver. Rather than planning out the route to begin with, Collins suggests that those leaders whose companies go from good to great begin with a relentless focus on personnel: "they start by getting the right people on the bus, the wrong people off the bus, and the right people in the right seats."[5] Collins asserts that there are "wrong people" and "mediocre people," who need to be jettisoned, quickly, if the organisation is going to succeed. I have seen this type of leadership operating in education, but I think it undermines the notion of a growth mindset.

The reason why I feel Collins' bus metaphor is unhelpful has its root in Gladwell's "Talent Myth." At its core, it implies that people are "right" or "wrong" or "mediocre." It does not countenance the possibility that people can *change*. Certainly, when I recruit new employees for my school, I am looking for talented individuals. I am also looking for those who understand the vision and values that the school holds and whose own vision and values align to those of the organisation. But unless you are in the rare position of starting a new school from scratch, when you start a new leadership role in education, you will inherit your predecessor's team and the organisation's pre-existing staff. In Collins' model, your next move would be to evaluate all of those pre-existing colleagues and remove those "wrong" people as quickly as possible. Not only is this approach potentially callous, but it is also prone to huge error and waste.

That is not to say that colleagues who are underperforming should be left alone. Far from it – the underperformance of one teacher undermines the effort of the whole, acting as a drag anchor which pulls the organisation back as it tries to make forward progress. But rather than jettisoning that colleague and leaving them behind, I have always believed it is far better to get under the skin of the problem to try and address it. Nobody would come to work in a school with the intention of making children less clever or holding them back, of preventing them from achieving. It's too much of an investment in time, training, personality, and energy for that level of perversity to be sustained. If we assume, then, that everyone working in the school is there for the right reasons – to help children to achieve – why is there underperformance? What are the underlying issues? What can be done about them? Working to support struggling colleagues is every leader's imperative. They must not be left behind; remember the team's time is taken from the slowest rider. It is the responsibility of everyone in the organisation to support one another to keep up the standard to which we all aspire.

Kev Bartle, Headteacher, gave a presentation on this topic at Canon's High School which has always stuck with me. In his thought-provoking presentation style, he decluttered his PowerPoint slides, removing all words and instead just displaying a single image to illustrate his ideas. He described how, in his early days of leadership, he was advised to tend to the garden of his staff by lavishing his attention on those who were new to the profession, those who were still learning and growing, at the expense of those old staffroom hands who had been teaching for thirty years or more and looked with long-suffering scepticism at the "new" initiatives coming round for the second or even third time in their careers. To illustrate this, he showed an image of stony, barren ground, reminiscent of the Parable of the Sower.[6] "Water the seedlings," he was advised, "but don't waste your water on the rocks." But, Kev explained, if you do water the rocks, something wonderful might just happen. And he clicked on to the next slide, a tiny green shoot poking up through the middle of an expanse of tarmac. And then, without further commentary, a glorious image of a tree that had split a rock completely in half, growing up through the boulder from the subsoil below. This rabbit-from-the-hat moment, delivered with all the aplomb of a teacher at the top of his game, has stayed with me ever since.

Collins' approach of getting the "wrong people" off the bus has, too often in my experience, been taken to mean getting rid of those old hands in the staffroom who have given twenty or thirty years' service to the school. They are seen as too set in their ways, too resistant to change, blockers, and naysayers. But the growth-minded leader should be alert to dissonant voices. "If colleagues who have been in teaching much longer than I have are resistant to this change," the growth mindset voice should say, "there must be a reason. Perhaps it's inertia, stubbornness, or even laziness. Perhaps. But what if – just *what if* – they are right and I am wrong? What then?"

This is the question that I constantly ask myself. Those colleagues with a decade or more experience on top of my own were godsends to me as a newly qualified teacher, offering me the benefit of their wisdom and saving me from wasted effort with workload-saving tips, classroom management advice, and effective techniques and shortcuts learned and honed through years upon years of dedicated, careful classroom practice. Why, now that I have been teaching for twenty years myself, should I now think that I know better than somebody who has been teaching for thirty? Should I not, rather, continue to learn from them? Listen to them? And, above all, *invest* in them? Those teachers are paid the most, often at the top of their pay scale and happy to stay in the classroom. They are the backbone of the school. They need nurture just as much as those new to the profession, and they have so much wisdom to offer. Rather than showing them the exit, maybe you should be handing them the map and asking them to help you navigate?

This focus on people is so important to me as Headteacher that when I started at Churchill Academy & Sixth Form, I set aside time to meet every single member of staff. With more than 150 on the books, it took me nearly four months to see them all – but it was the most vital investment of time I could have made. I asked everyone the same five questions, published in advance:

- What have you achieved over the past year?
- What do you hope to achieve over the next year?
- What are the best things about working at the Academy?
- What do you think the issues are?
- If you were me, what would you be working on?

I used these sessions to help me find out about the strengths, weaknesses, opportunities, and threats facing the Academy, but also to find out about the people who worked there. Who were they? What made them tick? What were their enthusiasms, their interests, their passions, their frustrations? It helped me to shape the vision – more of which later – but it also, vitally, established relationships with the colleagues who I had been appointed to lead. It enabled me to ask them about the projects they were working on, both personal and professional, and to greet every colleague by name with a smile. It helped me to understand the crucial role that every individual played in the functioning of the whole, from the pastoral leaders to the site staff, the science technicians to the school nurse, the receptionists to the senior leaders – each, in some way, relied on the others to be able to do their job effectively. The interrelation between the roles, and the individuals within those roles, was what would make or break the success of the school. Where it was most effective, the roles and relationships were clearly defined, and the individuals within those roles trained and able to do them well. Where there were issues, the solution was not to throw the person off the bus, but to ensure the role and relationship was defined and the individual properly trained so they were able to match up to the high expectations I had of every colleague. And my role was to watch the whole thing, providing the feedback and nudges to make sure that everything ran in time, in the same direction, and bang on the schedule we'd set ourselves.

We and us, not me and I: the headteacher as conductor

My second issue with the bus-as-metaphor-for-leading-a-school is the idea that there is one person in the driving seat. This is not my vision for school leadership. It is far more like the team pursuit, where everyone has their time driving the team forward, where everyone has a contribution to make. The organisation only thrives when everyone works together. That is why, in all my communications as Headteacher, I only ever use the first person plural. I only ever talk about projects that *we* are working on, about changes that *we* are making, about achievements that *we* are proud of. That sense of collective responsibility is carried by the language, but felt in the culture.

The bus driver, then, is not the image that I would choose for the headteacher. But, if I am to have a role on Jim Collins' bus, then I am old enough to remember the days when buses were crewed by two: the driver and the conductor. And the role of the conductor is a far more apposite image for how I envisage the growth-minded headteacher than that of the driver.

There is another image of the headteacher as conductor that I return to repeatedly. Benjamin Zander, the conductor of The Boston Philharmonic Orchestra, was 45 years old, already twenty years into his conducting career, when he realised: "The conductor of an orchestra doesn't make a sound. My picture appears on the front of the CD, but the conductor doesn't make a sound. He depends for his power on his ability to make other people powerful."[7] Like the team pursuit coach, the conductor is not the one performing, but the conductor enables and motivates the performance. The conductor provides continual feedback to the orchestra, keeping everyone in time and together towards the shared vision of the piece, investing the written score – the blueprint for the performance – with the emotion and drive which lifts it from the page and makes it real. As with the team pursuit, you can't drop a rider: every note in every part counts towards the sound of the whole. Therefore the conductor needs to pay just as much attention to the third violins as to the percussion, as much to the clarinets as the cellos, and as much to the tuba as the piccolo. Everybody counts. It's an inclusive vision of leadership which, again, does not rely on superstars but depends on every single person working together towards the shared whole, refining the performance through individual practice and group rehearsal, until all move as one.

To get this relationship to work effectively, as Headteacher I need to maintain that overview and keep my eyes everywhere in the school, just as the conductor scans the orchestra before the next big cue. I need to be on top of the performance of every aspect of the school. There are many ways of doing this. Of course, monitoring the data coming out of the assessments helps track the outcomes of students. Development review meetings with teams and individuals emphasise celebrating success, but also frankly and honestly confront difficulty and struggle so that we can look together for solutions. There are those formal self-evaluation activities which leadership manuals give you templates for, generating RAG-rated grids and dashboards and reports. These all have their place. But for me, every day, I have a half-hour slot in my diary labelled "walk the school." At that point in the day, no matter what else is happening, I get out and walk the corridors, popping in to lessons, stopping off in offices and workrooms, visiting studios and workshops and laboratories and sports fields to see what's happening. I don't make any notes. I don't record it in any other way than in forming an impression of how things are going. But I get out there and see the moving parts in motion, meshing and turning, driving the school forwards. I speak to the students, find out what they're working on, and talk to them about the progress they are making. I do this every day, without fail, and over time I get the "feel" for the school, its beating heart, its tempo and its rhythm. Every interaction I have is informed by this feedback loop, as I am able to make those adjustments needed to keep everything working in time, together, towards that common goal.

Learning leadership

CPD is one of those acronyms bandied around in educational circles with great freedom. Yet the idea of *continuing* professional development is one that goes to the core of growth mindset for educators, and that certainly includes leadership. You need to accept, as Dylan Wiliam once said, that "this job of teaching is so hard that one lifetime isn't enough to master it."[8]

If, as I presupposed earlier, we do not compete with one another as professionals, we must instead push ourselves to be better than our previous best. There will be others who are better at what we do than we are; our mission then is to learn from them so we can do it better too, not so we can do it better than them. Thus, leadership, like teaching, is a set of learned behaviours honed over time through practice and feedback. In education, of course, leaders are trained as teachers in the first place, and they learn the skills of leadership in the classroom. But in roles where leadership is the main focus, specific development is required. Leaders, like students, need to be growth minded about their leadership, accepting that the work of improvement in leadership skills is never finished.

In order to carry on this process of learning leadership, we require the same sort of feedback that students need about their work in class: kind, specific, and helpful. The problem with this kind of feedback is that it flows against the hierarchical relationship. In the classroom, the teacher is positioned above the students in the hierarchy, and therefore feedback flows naturally down the line from teacher to student. The student is expecting it, even wanting it; the teacher naturally understands that it is their role to provide it. The same is true in the traditional performance development process: the line manager observes the teacher in class and provides feedback. The teacher is expecting it, even wanting it; the line manager understands that it is their role to provide it. Yet to receive feedback on our *leadership*, the feedback must flow in the other direction, up the hierarchy from the led to the leader. There is a risk in this process in that the feedback may not be as honest as we would like – or, perhaps, a little too honest for our liking. The imbalance in the relationship creates pressures on the situation that can make it difficult for the managed to provide honest and objective feedback on the manager. But it is the leader's role to invite that feedback and to create the culture where they are showing that they not only expect that kind of feedback, but actively seek it so that they can do their job better. It can be done anonymously, through a "suggestion box" approach or any one of a number of online tools to obtain 360° feedback on practice. Once the feedback is collected, of course, the growth-minded leader must be open to receiving it – even if it is critical. Inviting and validating that approach, thanking colleagues for feedback which is challenging, helps to build a growth mindset in leadership. Without it, schools can enter into a "groupthink" culture, a kind of echo chamber where ideas, once floated, are validated by those around them simply because the leader has had the idea. "If they've come up with it," the prevailing wisdom goes, "it can't possibly be wrong." This is neither healthy nor, of course, accurate. Leaders are just as prone to fallibility – and stupid ideas – as the next person. Asking "why might this not work?" or inviting a colleague to play devil's advocate as ideas are discussed can be helpful ways of guarding against a groupthink culture.

Equally, when things do go wrong – as they often do in schools – the growth-minded leader's first reaction should never be about blame. This is frighteningly common and, I fear, becoming more so as high-stakes accountability builds pressure on schools and their leaders. A slip in results can be devastating, but it is the leader's responsibility to remember that the teachers concerned did not set out with the intention of ruining young people's life chances by wrecking their GCSE results. Rather, those teachers did their best to ensure that the children did well – but, despite those best intentions, they did not succeed. Why was this? What went wrong? What were the issues? And why – crucially – did the leaders not spot it in time? It's easy to blame the teachers. But in a growth mindset school, we all share the responsibility for success. Our time is taken from the slowest rider, and it is the responsibility of all of us to ensure that everyone keeps up with the pace. If one department has poor results one year, responsibility lies with all of us for not seeing it and not doing something about it sooner. So the growth-minded leader does not go in with blame and recrimination, but with support and help. As Megan Tschannen-Moran puts it: "There is no passing the buck, no scapegoating, no pointing fingers at others. This means the willingness to accept responsibility not just for good things that happen, but for mistakes and negative outcomes as well."[9]

Trust leadership

The work of Megan Tschannen-Moran, Professor of Educational Leadership at the William and Mary School of Education in Williamsburg, Virginia, is among the most interesting research in the field of educational leadership at the moment. Her research into leadership in schools is centred on the relationships of trust in school settings and how these are related to important outcomes such as the collective efficacy beliefs of a school faculty, teacher professionalism, and student achievement.[10]

What Tschannen-Moran's research[11] shows is an understanding of schools as complex systems where simple explanations of cause and effect are next to impossible due to the sheer number of variables in operation at any one time. Anyone who teaches knows this to be true. The cast-iron lesson which has succeeded in rendering a complex concept understandable the last three times you taught it to three different classes can suddenly fail with a new class, maybe because it's period five instead of a morning lesson, or maybe because it's a windy day, or maybe because a particular student had a falling-out at break time and arrives intent on continuing their issue in the classroom – if any one of a number of moving parts within the lesson goes awry, it can start a chain reaction which can unsettle, unbalance, and ultimately derail the learning. If this is true within a lesson, multiplying that up to school level can create such a level of complexity that it can be hard to trace impact back to source at all. You *think* that the change you made to the assessment system has had an impact on improving student scores year-on-year, but maybe it was just that the different cohorts of students you had in the school in those particular years were already predisposed to success in those particular topics. You *think* that the Maths Department have done particularly well with disadvantaged boys in Year 7 this year, but maybe there was a change in Year 6 teacher in two of your primary schools and the Maths team are benefitting from the increased progress made by the end of Key Stage 2. In short, in complex systems such as schools, policy change is never likely to have a simple and linear outcome as there are so many other variables in play.

Tschannen-Moran argues that in order to effect change in a complex organisation such as a school, the relationships between the component parts of the system need to be founded on trust, and that trust in a principal (or headteacher in the UK context) has an indirect but significant predictive impact on student achievement. If teachers trust their headteacher, their students do better. Trust acts as a kind of "glue" holding the organisation together and enabling improvements in practice to be enacted through the affiliation, autonomy, and agency[12] of the teachers in the classroom. The headteacher does not have a direct impact on student achievement, but through trust, their behaviour can enable and amplify their indirect effect.

Through her research, she has also codified the behaviours which can develop and maintain these elements of trust into five areas: vulnerability, benevolence, honesty, openness, and competence. The interrelation of these five qualities form a complex system of their own and, as with all aspects of leadership, are not fixed constructs but subject to development, improvement, and change. In particular, openness and vulnerability require the leader to demonstrate the ability to listen to and act on constructive critique in order to continue to improve. Leaders that demonstrate these five qualities are more likely to get "buy-in" from their teachers and, subsequently, multiply their impact in the classroom – an effect that Tschannen-Moran describes as "collective teacher efficacy." Trust in leadership builds a positive environment for the teachers, which in turn creates a positive environment for the students, with the ultimate impact of creating "vibrant schools."[13]

Implementing growth mindset leadership

Developing growth-mindset leadership in a school comes down to the culture and expectations that the organisation holds. As Deputy Head and then Headteacher in a secondary school, it is down to me to model the expectations that I have of others.

That means me being vulnerable, benevolent, honest, open, and competent in my role, and expecting those same behaviours of my colleagues. At the same time, it requires demonstrating that we are all continuously improving in our practice as leaders, just as we continue to improve our teaching, and our students continue to improve their levels of achievement in the classroom. As leaders, I expect all of us to be open to feedback and critique, and to deliberately practice our leadership skills, taking time to focus on developing those aspects of our leadership which can improve the impact that we have on others.

At the same time the impact of that leadership requires a clear sense of expectation, laid out and shared as the priorities for the school – our vision statement. When compiling the vision for Churchill Academy & Sixth Form, we tried to imagine the school we would be if we got every aspect of our practice right, if every part of the machine was firing on all cylinders, and if the ethos and culture we wanted to create was implemented. We initially compiled the following series of descriptors:

1. To promote the welfare of students and staff

   What does this look like?

   - All students have access to personalised pathways through the curriculum and access to appropriate support.

   - All members of the Academy are regarded as individuals: "treat people as people."

   - Barriers to success are identified and overcome.

   - The Academy has a sense of family, belonging, and enjoyment.

   - Achievement in all activities is recognised and celebrated.

   - High-quality staff are recruited and retained across the Academy.

   - There is equality of opportunity and respect for all members of the community, celebrating diversity.

2. To develop the very best practice in teaching, learning and leadership

   What does this look like?

   - Leadership

     - A leadership development programme is established and effective.

     - Classroom teachers are empowered to lead innovation within the classroom.

     - Students are empowered in the leadership of learning.

     - Churchill works in collaboration with other schools and educational settings to develop leadership across the system.

- Teaching and learning

  - There is a single-minded focus on improving classroom practice: a mantra of "learn at all costs."

  - Students demonstrate a hunger for learning, taking responsibility for their own progress and development.

  - All staff are accessing professional development which improves their practice.

  - Staff develop and share best practice, learning from one another to create a cycle of continuous improvement.

3. To develop a growth mindset across the Academy, so that learners embrace challenges, persist in the face of setbacks, and see effort as the path to success

   What does this look like?

   - Learners set themselves ambitious goals and are not limited by their prior attainment, taking responsibility and embracing struggle.

   - Learners challenge themselves to achieve their best: "if it's not excellent, it's not finished."

   - Students have an independent work ethic which renders catch up and extra sessions redundant.

   - Learning focuses on the process over the product.

   - Learners receive effective feedback that is acted upon and has an impact.

   - Robust performance development processes ensure that all staff continuously improve their practice.

   - Systems within the Academy align with a growth mindset ethos.

   - Students model successful learning attitudes and behaviours across the Academy: "don't stop until you're proud."

4. To set consistently high expectations so that all learners achieve exceptional personal and academic outcomes

   What does this look like?

   - Academic outcomes

     - Significantly positive outcomes against national benchmarks.

     - Outcomes improving year-on-year.

- Gaps between groups closing year-on-year.

- Excellent progress from all starting points.

- Students progress to secure and aspirational destinations including top universities, apprenticeships, and employment.

- Personal outcomes

  - Students display consistently excellent attitudes and behaviour for learning.

  - Character, resilience, and employability skills are developed through curricular and extra-curricular activities.

  - Students make a valuable contribution to the community to develop their citizenship and spiritual, moral, and social education.

In this set of descriptions, we captured aspects of the kind of school we wanted to work in. From this point, we worked with our staff, students, and governors to develop our Academy vision statement. Under the core purpose – "to inspire and enable young people to make a positive difference" – we laid out our vision for learning: "to set no limits on what we can achieve."

At Churchill Academy & Sixth Form we believe in the value of:

- Determined and consistent effort

- A hunger to learn new things

- Challenging ourselves to go beyond what is comfortable

- Viewing setbacks and mistakes as opportunities to learn and grow

- Seeking and responding to feedback

- Encouraging others to succeed

This vision encapsulates the features that we want at Churchill as a growth mindset school. Each team within the Academy – the senior leadership team, each faculty, each pastoral team, all of the support staff teams – focus their action plans on how they are going to help to move the Academy towards the vision laid out in descriptors. And each individual within the organisation sets themselves an area of focus that will shift the school further towards that vision, which develops them as professionals and makes a contribution towards the whole. That way, every action and initiative within the school is aligned towards the realisation of that goal. Of course, we aren't there – yet. But having a higher-level goal, the grit and determination to change our practice, and the professionalism to work together towards that aim enables us to move closer to it in every single interaction inside and outside of every single lesson taught.

Notes

1 Tom Sherrington blogs at: https://teacherhead.com/
2 John Tomsett blogs at: https://johntomsett.com/
3 You can read my blog here: https://chrishildrew.wordpress.com/
4 Gladwell, "The talent myth."
5 Collins, "Good to great."

6 Behold, there went out a sower to sow: And it came to pass, as he sowed, some fell by the way side, and the fowls of the air came and devoured it up. And some fell on stony ground, where it had not much earth; and immediately it sprang up, because it had no depth of earth: But when the sun was up, it was scorched; and because it had no root, it withered away. And some fell among thorns, and the thorns grew up, and choked it, and it yielded no fruit. And other fell on good ground, and did yield fruit that sprang up and increased; and brought forth, some thirty, and some sixty, and some an hundred. And he said unto them, He that hath ears to hear, let him hear.

(Mark 4: 3–9)

7 Zander's keynote address to the National College of School Leaders was available on Teachers' TV. The archived version can be found in" Benjamin Zander: Gurus."
8 Wiliam, "How do we prepare our students."
9 Tschannen-Moran & Gareis, "Principals, trust, and cultivating vibrant schools," page 260.
10 Tschannen-Moran's website, home page.
11 For example, Tschannen-Moran & Gareis: "Faculty trust in the principal" and *Cultivating Vibrant Schools.*
12 The "three As" of effective leadership are suggested by Alan Maclean in *The Motivated School.*
13 Tschannen-Moran & Gareis, "Principals, trust, and cultivating vibrant schools."

Bibliography

Collins, J. (2001, October). Good to great. Retrieved 10 April, 2017, from Jim Collins' website: www.jimcollins.com/article_topics/articles/good-to-great.html
Dweck, C. (2012). *Mindset: How You Can Fulfil Your Potential.* London: Robinson.
Gladwell, M. (2002, 22 July). The talent myth. Retrieved 9 April, 2017, from *The New Yorker*: www.newyorker.com/magazine/2002/07/22/the-talent-myth
Mclean, A. (2003). *The Motivated School.* London: Sage Publications Ltd.
Tschannen-Moran, M. (2016, 31 December). Home page. Retrieved 10 April, 2017, from *Megan Tschannen-Moran's website*: http://wmpeople.wm.edu/site/page/mxtsch/home
Tschannen-Moran, M., & Gareis, C.R. (2015, February). Faculty trust in the principal: An essential ingredient in high-performing schools. *Journal of Education Adminstration*, *53*(1), 66–92.
Tschannen-Moran, M., & Gareis, C.R. (2015). Principals, trust, and cultivating vibrant schools. *Societies*, *5*, 256–276.
Wiliam, D. (2012, 5 December). *How do we prepare our students for a world we cannot possibly imagine?* Keynote address: *SSAT National Conference*, Liverpool.
Zander, B. (2006, 10 July). Benjamin Zander: Gurus. Retrieved 10 April, 2017, from *TeachFind*: http://archive.teachfind.com/ttv/www.teachers.tv/videos/benjamin-zander.html

7 A growth mindset curriculum

The curriculum is the core of any school. Decisions about what you are going to teach and how you are going to teach it are fundamental to the success of the whole endeavour. In order to discuss this fully, it is perhaps helpful to separate these two elements out. In this chapter I will discuss the curriculum (*what* we teach) and the structures (*how* we teach it).

The curriculum

One common misconception I often encounter in the discussion of growth mindset is that you either have one or you don't. As I suggested in Chapter 5, almost everyone who takes a mindset questionnaire comes out somewhere along a continuum between completely fixed mindset and completely growth mindset. We all have elements of growth and fixed mindsets in our psychological make-up. However, it is also important to remember that our mindsets can be very domain-specific. As Dweck herself says: "nobody has a growth mindset in everything all the time. Everyone is a mixture of fixed and growth mindsets."[1] Thus it is entirely possible for students to approach their PE with a growth mindset but believe that they will never be any good at maths, or for them to spend hours working on a single dance move to perfect it whilst at the same time giving up in frustration on their art project. Recognising this renders the application of questionnaire scores across the curriculum problematic at best, and healthy caution should be used when suggesting that a student "has a growth mindset" in a generic sense.

Why should this be? In my experience of education, I have heard repeatedly about the idea of "transferable skills" such as critical thinking, problem-solving, or evaluation. Shouldn't a growth mindset be transferable in the same way? The answer, of course, is that the notion of transferable skills which can be taught in a decontextualised way is a chimera. In order for anyone to think critically or solve a problem, they need something to think about and a specific problem to solve. They require *knowledge* – key information about the topic, often including background and context, and usually procedural knowledge which includes the steps that could be taken to resolve a problem. In order to evaluate anything, knowledge is required not only of the item under evaluation but also of comparable similar items, their qualities, and composition. A growth mindset is exactly the same. It isn't just about trying harder and applying more effort. A growth mindset requires knowledge of the strategies and processes which are likely to be effective in learning within a particular subject. Without that knowledge, effort is likely to be fruitless and ineffective, and the application of fruitless and ineffective effort is disheartening and off-putting.

This phenomenon can be likened to the Matthew effect. This phenomenon takes its name from the Parable of the Talents in the Book of Matthew.[2] In the parable, a master who was leaving his house to travel entrusted his property to his three servants. According to the abilities of each man, one servant received five talents, the second servant received two talents, and the third servant received one talent. (A talent, in Biblical terms, was a mass of gold equivalent to about 130 pounds.) Upon returning home, after a long absence, the master asked his three servants for an account of the talents he had entrusted to them. The first and second servants explained that they each put their talents to work and doubled their value, presenting the master with ten and four talents respectively. These servants were rewarded. The third servant, however, had buried his talent in the ground, fearful of losing it or damaging it. He returned it and it alone. The master was angry, and he took the single talent from the third servant, giving it instead to the first servant to add to his ten, and cast the third servant out of his household.

Matthew concludes:

> For the one who has will be given more, and he will have more than enough. But the one who does not have, even what he has will be taken from him. And throw that worthless slave into the outer darkness, where there will be weeping and gnashing of teeth.[3]

The Matthew effect is used to describe situations where those that have plenty will gain more, whilst those who have little, lose even that. In Daniel Rigney's book of the same name, the phenomenon is explored across society and specifically in educational terms in learning to read. Rigney says: "good readers gain new skills very rapidly, and quickly move from 'learning to read' to 'reading to learn,' [whilst] poor readers become increasingly frustrated with the act of reading, and try to avoid reading where possible."[4] In other words, those "poor readers" who start with little vocabulary, grammar, phonic, or syntax knowledge rapidly enter a fixed mindset state where they decide they either "can't read" or "won't read," avoiding the situation which will expose their weakness and therefore protecting their self-image and self-worth. Clearly, this is a self-defeating strategy, as the best way to improve reading is to practise it, and by denying themselves that practice, the poor readers fall further and further behind the good readers.

Rigney's proposition goes further, of course, by aligning the skill of learning to read with the advantage that it confers to other aspects of the curriculum. The ability to read allows children to access learning in other areas and to acquire content and procedural knowledge in other domains. The growth in learning for those good readers is potentially exponential, whilst those poor readers who have avoided practice and struggle to decode are denied access to additional learning. Their disadvantage in reading soon confers disadvantage on other aspects of learning, inculcating the same fixed mindset across the curriculum. "To the one that has will be given more . . . but the one who does not have, even what he has will be taken from him." It is easy to see how this disenfranchisement from learning can be equated to being thrown "into the outer darkness," and the "weeping and gnashing of teeth" is understandable.

Whilst this is clearly true of reading, it is also the case for knowledge more widely. For our students to think critically, solve problems, and evaluate, they need a wide range of background knowledge related to the domains in which they are applying those skills. For example, if I want the students in my English class to think critically about a poem and evaluate the poet's use of figurative language, they will need to be able not only to read the poem – to decode the letters into phonemes, sounds, and words linked to meanings stored in their long-term memory – but also to draw on their knowledge of different types of figurative language that could be used. On top of that, they will need to make comparative judgments about the originality, the appropriateness, and perhaps the vividness of the language used. To do this, they will need to draw on the bank of other poems they have read, also stored in their long-term memory, to establish whether or not the metaphor they are looking at is a good one or not. The more poems the students have read, the better their ability to make that kind of critical evaluation. "To the one that has will be given more."

The same is true across the curriculum. Take History, for example. We might wish to teach the skill of evaluating sources. This is doubtless a worthy aim, and we would all want our historians to be able to evaluate a source for its reliability, validity, possible biases, and veracity. The only way to accomplish this, however, is with as much background knowledge about the historical period and context as it is possible to bring to bear. When faced with an account of a Luddite riot, I would be ill-equipped to conduct such an evaluation without detailed knowledge of early nineteenth-century politics and industrial history, some key names, dates and locations, and information about the movement's aims and methods. If I had this knowledge, however, the new source that I was evaluating would also slot into the knowledge bank that I had around the Luddite movement, further enriching my understanding of the period and allowing me to make still more sophisticated evaluations in the future. "To the one that has will be given more." Without the context, I would not be able to place the source in relation to other knowledge, and I would therefore be less likely to remember it in future.

So what is to be done? In planning the curriculum, thought must be given to the knowledge that students should be taught. This is a difficult area, often politicised and subject to a discussion of values and influence.[5] However, primarily, it is essential that students have the background knowledge to be able fully to understand what they are reading and learning about. If we take reading as an example, our students need to know what the writers assume is already known and, therefore, do not explain in their writing. In a Jane Austen novel, that might include gender roles and the implications of social class in nineteenth-century England, as well as the names for different types of horse-drawn carriages. In reading a newspaper article about the US Presidential election, it might include knowledge about the different political stances of the two main parties, an understanding of the roles of Congress and the Senate, and the functioning of the primaries in selecting candidates. Whatever it is that students are learning about, they need sufficient background knowledge to be able to contextualise the new knowledge they are being taught, connect it to the things they already know, and by doing so, secure it in their long-term memory.

Without consideration of the knowledge demands of new learning, the curriculum risks inculcating a fixed mindset in learners. At the same time, each subject, or "domain," should be planned individually in relation to the knowledge content that is required to be successful in that subject. What is it that we want our students to know about science, about maths, about art and music? Or, more pertinently, what is that we *need* students to know about these subjects? These are what Daniel Willingham calls the "unifying ideas of each discipline."[6] These fundamental concepts recur again and again within subjects and should be taught early, and returned to often. In Maths, for example, these unifying ideas might include numeracy, place value, the base 10 system, and arithmetic and proportional reasoning.

Vitally, then, new learning needs to be connected to prior learning so that it is meaningful and adds to the store of knowledge already accrued. They cannot put the stained glass in the windows of their cathedral without the frame for that window; that window sits in a wall, which is supported by a foundation and connected, hopefully, to a spectacular buttress that supports the vaulted roof. What are the foundation stones of your subject? What are the bricks of the south wall? What are the crenellations that top your subject off? Where does it end?

These fundamental curriculum questions might seem far-reaching. However, if we truly want students to have a growth mindset, we need to ensure that the path through that learning is structured. The new learning within the curriculum needs to be challenging – students should struggle to learn it – but it should be achievable within the construct and context of the learning that they have already acquired. It should all be part of building the cathedral.

In practical terms, once the whole-school principles of a knowledge-based curriculum have been established, it is crucial that subject experts establish both the unifying ideas within the discipline and the knowledge that students will need in order to be successful in that discipline. This body of knowledge then needs structuring into a coherent programme across the student's experience in a school. I have been guilty of planning schemes of work a unit at a time, perhaps a year at a time, or a key stage at a time, without looking up to see the overview. What does this unit contribute to the student's overall experience within this subject discipline? How is it helping to build expertise? In that sense, curriculum planning has been very much like the road-builders in the forest.

In this parable, described by Stephen Covey,[7] a group of workers and their leaders are set a task of clearing a road through a dense jungle on a remote island. Their task is to get to the coast, where an estuary provides a perfect site for a port. The leaders organise the workers into efficient teams and ensure that equipment, tools, and materials are distributed quickly to the teams as required. Progress is excellent. The leaders continue to monitor and evaluate progress, making adjustments along the way to ensure the progress is maintained and efficiency increased wherever possible. Then, one day, amidst all the hustle and bustle and activity, one worker climbs up a nearby tree. The worker surveys the scene from the top of the tree and shouts down to the assembled group below: "Wrong way!" This is the risk of curriculum planning, or indeed any activity, without a sense of overview.

For that reason, the notion of "key stages" within schools can be unhelpful dividers in planning the curriculum. My context has always been within secondary schools starting in Year 7, working with both a two-year and a three-year Key Stage 3 in various contexts. Whilst the key stage divide can be helpful as a marker for students choosing options and personalising their curriculums in certain ways, the curriculum plan should span the entire period of time that students could be studying it. It should take in the transition to further study post-16, including the A-level curriculum as appropriate. It should certainly look back to the primary curriculum to ensure that the knowledge base is consistent and the roadmap across the subject discipline is coherent across the transition. I am envious of all-through schools with the facility to adopt curriculum planning from 3 to 19; this provides the consistency that can be lacking in the transition from primary to secondary education. The development of cross-phase multi-academy trusts which incorporate primary and secondary schools provides an alternative vehicle to achieve this coherence and consistency of vision and direction.

Preparing students for exams

Of course, in any curriculum plan, it pays to be mindful of the external assessment system that the curriculum is preparing students for. Most likely, the unifying ideas of the discipline and the background knowledge required to be successful in it will cross over with an examination specification in that subject. However, curriculum planning should not be dictated by the assessment regime. Across the secondary curriculum there is enough space, time, and flexibility to establish curriculum content *beyond* the examination specifications. Planning should start with the question "what do we want the children to know and be able to do?" and continue from that point.

Simply put, it is the difference between teaching a student to pass exams in languages, history or science and teaching students to be linguists, historians, or scientists. Over recent years, students have been able to rote-learn passages of Spanish or French to parrot back verbatim in their speaking or writing controlled assessments, without actually understanding the language they are learning. This has usually been enough to achieve a passing grade in those subjects. But is this really the business of education? This approach renders the subject inconsequential, leads to shallow learning which is not retained beyond the assessment for which it has been memorised, and, crucially, fixes the mindset of the learner. The hidden message of this kind of approach to languages is: "we don't think you're capable of actually learning French, so just memorise this and it will be enough to get you through." It does not encourage students to be learners. And it does not encourage them to be linguists.

In this sense, the move to a fully examined system is a positive one. The system of coursework and controlled assessment, coupled with an accountability system which encouraged schools and teachers to push students over the C/D borderline and no more, entrenched these approaches within schools. Learning without understanding was enough to get you by: "You just need to know this; you don't need to understand it. As soon as the controlled assessment is done, you don't need to worry about this – or remember it – any more." Such a system devalued learning and militated against the growth mindset in schools. It encouraged students into an environment where they were required to "look smart" for one assessment, but not actually to learn. Although a terminal examination system places significant pressure on single-take assessments, it does create an environment which values learning, retention, and recall – all aspects in which a growth mindset will help students succeed. If we educate our young people to be linguists, historians, and scientists, terminal examinations in languages, history and science should not be seen as a threat, but as an opportunity to show what they can do.

At this point, it's also worth thinking about the approach and the attitude we take towards tests and exams across the curriculum. Cognitive science has shown[8] that practice testing is one of the most effective ways not just of assessing learning, but securing it. The act of retrieving information from the long-term memory, processing it in relation to a question, and reshaping it into new forms seems to strengthen and secure the pathways to that information in the mind. It also identifies gaps in learning so that teachers and students can address them in future. In short: it's a highly effective technique. The problem arises from an academic culture which emphasises the grade or mark achieved on the test rather than the process of taking the test and learning from it. This is classic fixed mindset thinking, where the student's reaction on receiving their test back is to turn to their neighbour and ask "what did you get?" It has been reinforced by the years of controlled assessment culture in which the outcome of the test "counted" towards the final grade and the product mattered much more than the process. For the effectiveness of testing as a learning tool to be realised, this must be flipped so that tests are seen as part of the process of learning, not as a product. In fact, the only time the product "counts" is in the final GCSE or A-level exams at the end of a course. Every other test, mock exam, quiz, assessment, or assignment is part of the process of learning. Yes, it's important that students try their best on them, use the test as an actual test, revise, and prepare; but in a growth mindset school, the point of taking the test is not to show other people how smart you are, but to learn from it yourself.

In building this approach to tests and exams, I have found that being explicit about their purpose from the outset definitely helps. This includes being clear with students and with their families as well as with staff. For most adults, tests are inextricably linked to a high-stakes, performance-driven system. This understanding of what tests are, and what they are for, can easily be transmitted through expectations and reactions when tests are set, when they are taken, and when feedback is given. The only way to reverse this cultural inheritance is to deliberately, explicitly, and repeatedly unpick it, emphasising the learning outcome again and again. Ensuring regular, low-stakes tests and quizzes to check understanding and secure learning can be part of the curriculum planning, but ensuring that their delivery emphasises learning should be part of every teacher's responsibility. I will deal with this approach further in Chapter 10.

Curriculum structures

Once the curriculum content has been established and planned, the structures within which it will be delivered need to be addressed. In the growth mindset school that means first and foremost tackling the idea of how students are to be grouped into classes and how those classes will be timetabled.

The grouping of students by ability is widespread across British schools. Every school I have worked in, and certainly the school I went to, used ability grouping to some extent, and this seems to be a representative sample in relation to the experience of others. And yet the evidence seems to indicate that grouping students by ability, whilst it has some benefit to the highest-attaining students, may actually disadvantage middle- and lower-attaining students. In its briefing based on "evidence on setting and streaming ... accumulated over at least 30 years of research,"[9] the Education Endowment Foundation's toolkit suggests that the overall impact of setting or streaming is negative by one month per year on student progress. That is to say, students in ability groups are, on average, a month behind those taught in mixed ability groups after one year of study. The Foundation's website summarises the research as follows:

> Low attaining learners who are set or streamed fall behind by 1 or 2 months per year, on average, when compared with the progress of similar students in classes with mixed ability groups. It appears likely that routine setting or streaming arrangements undermine low attainers' confidence and discourage the belief that attainment can be improved through effort.

[. . .] In contrast, studies show that higher attaining learners make between 1 and 2 additional months' progress when set or streamed compared to when taught in mixed ability groups.[10]

The language used here makes the link between grouping and mindset explicit. Setting students by ability can "discourage the belief that attainment can be improved through effort" – in other words, setting students puts them into a fixed mindset. It is easy to find the precedent for this in Dweck's own experience of being sat around her sixth-grade class in IQ order, and it is also easy to identify this in the daily experience of students up and down the country who say, "I can't get that grade, I'm only in set 2," or who identify themselves as a "set 5 kid" with the associated implication of underachievement, lack of aspiration, and, in all likelihood, challenging behaviour.

The issue arises as a result of labelling and its interplay with self-image. By placing a child in a group labelled "set 4 of 5," you automatically create a hierarchy of achievement and identify this child's place within that hierarchy. At that point in time, the child's performance is fixed at this particular point. It is, of course, possible to approach the situation with a growth mindset and to understand that this is one point in time. With deliberate practice and effort, with careful and consistent application of appropriate strategies and learning processes, it is entirely possible to improve performance over time. Being in set 4 now does not mean that you will be in set 4 forever. But, in most cases, the creation of this label puts a barrier in the way of a growth mindset and makes it more difficult to achieve. In my experience, most of the children put into set 5 in Year 7 are still in set 5 in Year 11.

That is not to say that teaching in mixed ability groups in any way removes the dangers of creating fixed mindset hierarchies. In fact, even in schools which apply rigorous setting and streaming procedures, every class is a mixed ability class. Teachers can often indulge in great rigmaroles to mask performance hierarchies within classes, but the students know where they are. They know who is doing well and who is finding it difficult, and they know, more or less, where they fit within the hierarchy. Most students will have this figured out within a few lessons in a new class. The aim, in any system, is to ensure that the children really believe that current performance is not a determining influence on future performance and that progress can be made as a result of applying deliberate effort to the learning tasks at hand. And the only way to instil this belief is to demonstrate its veracity through repeated experience. This means designing learning tasks so that students struggle, but have access to strategies and knowledge to address the difficulties they are facing, and so that they see the tangible progress they have made. Reinforcing this experience with praise for the effort and use of strategies which led to the progress, again and again, will build the self-belief that current performance levels are not fixed, but can be improved.

Can't this approach also be implemented within a system of setting or streaming? Of course it can. My argument is that there must be a concerted, focused effort to build a growth mindset approach through experiences of learning in whichever system of grouping is used, but that this effort is more important than ever in a system of setting or streaming which predisposes learners towards the fixed mindset. The same is true on a system level within schools which are in selective areas. Where selection for grammar school education takes place through the 11 plus examination, some students arrive at school in Year 7 already believing that they "can't do maths" or, indeed, anything, having already "failed" at the end of primary school. The battle to develop a growth mindset in a system stacked against it is more difficult – though not impossible – to win.

I have, so far, largely focused on the experience of the middle- or low-attaining students within the curriculum structures. However, as Dweck's own experience illustrates, the creation of ability-based hierarchies can have detrimental consequences on those at the upper end of the attainment scale as well. Certainly in my experience of developing growth mindset approaches in schools, higher-attaining students are highly susceptible to fixed mindsets too. A "set 1" label can induce a fear of failure which, in turn, can manifest as an unwillingness to try or a hesitation to commit anything to paper unless it is sure to be perfect. I have seen students as young as Year 7 rip out a page of their exercise book due to a single spelling mistake, as they do not want to have it blemished by a crossing-out. This could be a symptom of a genuine pride in presentation, but it is easy to see this crossing over into a fear of any kind of error or mistake.

Conversely, higher-attaining students can go through schooling without encountering genuine academic struggle until relatively late in their journey. These are the students who successfully navigate their primary and secondary education, grasping the curriculum placed before them quickly and performing well. They ace their tests, come close to the top of their year groups, are lauded with praise for their achievements, and are celebrated for their attainment. For them, the learning experience is one that they seem born to – you might argue that they have a "natural ability" for learning. This may well be the case. However, at some point as they continue with their studies, they will come across a topic, concept, subject, text, or problem that they are unable to grasp quickly and with the facility to which they have become accustomed. Bright, confident young people who have sailed contentedly through to the age of sixteen with something akin to ease, usually with a string of A and A* grades under their belt, suddenly come unstuck at the sight of their first D – or failing – grade. These students have built their self-image on being academically successful, but they have done so without ever really having to try and certainly without ever really having to struggle. And when the work gets hard, they don't have the strategies to fall back on. It's an alien experience. Suddenly, their academically successful self-image is in jeopardy, and the damage can take many months to repair.

For some, this happens at GCSE level, but in my experience it is more common as students make the transition to A-level. There are a few that I have taught in my career for whom the challenge did not kick in until undergraduate level, and

I can list a group of such students who dropped out of elite universities despite exemplary A-level results, unable to cope with the challenge of higher education. There is no doubt that the school curriculum – at which they were spectacularly successful – did not adequately prepare these students for further study. Rather, it praised and celebrated their intelligence and ability, fixing their mindsets and rendering them brittle and vulnerable when faced with academic struggle.

One of the arguments in favour of setting is that it allows teachers to stretch and challenge those higher-attaining students, sometimes called "gifted and talented" (although I will explain in Chapter 9 why I think referring to students in this way is a bad idea). This implies – possibly with some justification – that it is more difficult to do so in a class with all levels of attainment represented. Indeed, the Teaching and Learning Toolkit from the Education Endowment Fund[11] indicates that those higher-attaining learners make more progress in ability-set groups than they do when taught in the same classes as those with middle or low prior attainment, possibly due to this differentiation of the curriculum (although many other factors may contribute to this effect). Ofsted's 2013 report on *The Most Able Students* concluded that the performance of the brightest young people in non-selective schools required improvement because

> Many students become used to performing at a lower level than they are capable of. . . . Students did not do the hard work and develop the resilience needed to perform at a higher level because more challenging tasks were not regularly demanded of them. The work was pitched at the middle and did not extend the most able.[12]

All students need challenging tasks put in front of them if they are going to become successful learners and develop a growth mindset. Whether or not your particular school chooses to teach any particular subject in mixed ability sets, ability sets, bands, or streams, every student must have a curriculum which ensures that they are challenged as soon as it is possible to do so.

As a teacher, I used to be really proud of my students (and myself, for that matter) when they turned in perfect pieces of work. These were the students who received rewards, recognition, and praise aplenty. These were the books I would proudly show my colleagues and which my middle and senior leaders would be impressed by because they showed what excellent progress students were making. But now, as Headteacher, my thinking has changed. If I see a student who is able to complete a piece of work – not a presentation piece, but a piece of ongoing classwork – perfectly, getting every single question right, I am more likely to conclude that the student is not being sufficiently challenged. We should be aiming, in every lesson, with every student, to pitch it so that they are getting some of it wrong. Only then are they learning. In her RSA presentation, Carol Dweck reinforces this position, describing how to respond "if a child does something quickly and easily. Instead of rushing to tell them how good they are . . . we should say 'oh! I'm sorry I wasted your time. Let's do something hard. Let's do something you can learn from.'"[13]

I suppose it's a little like learning to drive, finding the biting point on the clutch which allows the car to move forward effectively. In this analogy, the car's engine is the curriculum and its delivery. It can be revved high, representing a high degree of challenge and higher academic level; or it can be revved low, representing a lower degree of challenge and increased accessibility. The students are the wheels of the car. The clutch is that linkage between the two, and it represents the degree of challenge with which the curriculum is presented to the students. Depress the clutch too far – set the level of challenge too low – and the engine will turn over at several thousand revolutions per minute without the car making any progress at all. Release the clutch too far or too fast – set the level of challenge too high – and the engine will stall. In this situation, we need to reset our expectation, restarting the engine of the lesson, before we can move forward together again. Similarly, if the engine is revving too fast or too slow, it won't matter how you release the clutch – the car will stall or bunny-hop, juddering to a halt. At the biting point, the curriculum pitch is just right, engaging with the students' prior understanding and attainment. There is some slippage, but enough friction to start to turn the wheels. As more of the curriculum engages, the clutch bites harder and the wheels speed up. Eventually, the clutch is released completely and the engine turns the wheels with full engagement. This is the mastery of that particular aspect of the curriculum. And then, of course, it's time for a higher gear.

With this kind of curriculum in place, the experience of schooling will change for those most able students. Rather than coasting through education, finding the experience easy until they hit a challenge which they are unable to overcome, they will become accustomed to struggle and difficulty. They will build resilience and grit, and they will be better equipped to tackle challenges which they encounter later in their academic or personal careers. But also, by finding that biting point earlier in their schooling and moving up through the gears throughout their education, they will make more progress. By working harder for longer, they will go further.

Notes

1 Carol Dweck interviewed by Christine Gross-Loh: "How praise became a consolation prize."
2 The Book of Matthew 25: 14–30.
3 Matthew 25: 29–30, New English Translation.
4 Rigney, *The Matthew Effect*, page 76.
5 The Matilda effect, for example, where the work of female scientists is often credited to men, can be cited as the influence of a patriarchal society on the history of science.
6 Willingham, *Why Don't Students Like School?*, page 48.
7 Covey. *The 7 Habits of Highly Effective People*.
8 Dunlosky, "Improving students' learning with effective learning techniques," and others.
9 Education Endowment Foundation, "Setting or streaming."

10 Ibid.
11 Ibid.
12 Ofsted, *The Most Able Students*, page 9.
13 Dweck, "How to help every child fulfil their potential."

Bibliography

Boaler, J., Wiliam, D., & Brown, M. (1998, 30 August). Students' experiences of ability grouping – disaffection, polarisation and the construction of failure. Retrieved 2 January, 2017, from the Centre for the Study of Mathematics Education, University of Nottingham: www.nottingham.ac.uk/csme/meas/papers/boaler.html

Covey, S. (2004). *The 7 Habits of Highly Effective People.* London: Simon & Schuster.

Dunlosky, J.E. (2013). Improving students' learning with effective learning techniques. *Psychological Science in the Public Interest, 14*(1), 4–58.

Dweck, C. (2015, 15 December). How to help every child fulfil their potential. Retrieved 23 December, 2016, from *The RSA*: https://www.thersa.org/discover/videos/rsa-animate/2015/how-to-help-every-child-fulfil-their-potential

Education Endowment Foundation. (2016, 1 August). Setting or streaming. Retrieved 1 January, 2017, from *Education Endowment Foundation* (Teaching and Learning Toolkit): https://educationendowmentfoundation.org.uk/resources/teaching-learning-toolkit/setting-or-streaming/

Gross-Loh, C. (2016, 16 December). How praise became a consolation prize. Retrieved 31 December, 2016, from *The Atlantic*: https://www.theatlantic.com/education/archive/2016/12/how-praise-became-a-consolation-prize/510845/

Hallam, S., Ireson, J., Lister, V., Chaudury, I. A., & Davies, J. (2003). Ability grouping in the primary school: A survey. *Educational Studies, 29*(1), 69–83.

Kutnick, P., Hodgkinson, S., Sebba, J., Humphreys, S., Galton, M., Steward, S., Blatchford, P., & Baines, E. (2006). *Pupil Grouping Strategies and Practices at Key Stage 2 and 3.* London: Department for Education and Skills.

Ofsted. (2013). *The Most Able Students.* London: Ofsted.

Rigney, D. (2010). *The Matthew Effect: How Advantage Begets Further Advantage.* New York: Columbia University Press.

Sukhnandan, L., & Lee, B. (1998). *Streaming, Setting and Grouping by Ability: A Review of the Literature.* Slough: NFER.

Willingham, D. T. (2009). *Why Don't Students Like School?* San Francisco: Jossey-Bass.

8 Attitude determines altitude

In Chapter 5, I discussed the NASA principle, introduced to me by Chris George, in which a janitor at Kennedy Space Center was able to articulate his contribution to the mission of putting a man on the moon. However, I also have NASA to thank for the title of this chapter. In 1996, NASA published their *Superstars of Spaceflight* booklet, part of their educational package designed to "encourage and inspire students and teachers to consider the expanded opportunities that await those who prepare themselves educationally as they pursue their dreams."[1]

I've always been taken with the use of this motto by an organisation responsible for space exploration. Within the field of flight dynamics, "attitude" is defined as the orientation of an aircraft or spacecraft, or the angle at which it is pointing. In that sense, the calculation of the correct attitude is essential for space flight to be successful. If the angle is too steep, the spacecraft will not have the power to achieve orbit, and it will stall and fall back to Earth. If the angle is too shallow, the spacecraft will not achieve enough height – or altitude – and will fall short of orbit. The attitude of a spacecraft or aircraft determines the altitude that it will reach. For once, it is not an analogy to say that this really is rocket science.

The other meaning of attitude is the one we are, perhaps, more familiar with. It is half a synonym with "mindset" itself: a settled way of thinking or feeling.[2] NASA recognised that the mental attitude with which it approached its goals was every bit as important as the scientific, engineering, and practical expertise. In fact, *Superstars of Spaceflight* was designed to celebrate and perpetuate the diversity of the space programme, noting the contributions of astronauts of all genders and ethnic origins to pushing the boundaries of human exploration. It does not, however, include one of my own personal heroes, the mathematician Katherine Johnson. This pioneer overcame the double prejudice against her gender and her skin colour to work on the space flight programme, calculating the trajectories for Alan Shepard's first American space flight and John Glenn's first orbit of the Earth, as well as the moon landings and, later, the space shuttle programme. Before her retirement, she even worked on the analytical geometry of a manned space mission to Mars.[3]

The moon landings themselves are, I think, an example of a growth mindset in action. President Kennedy's famous speech in Rice Stadium laid out the rationale for the space programme when he said:

> We choose to go to the moon. We choose to go to the moon in this decade and do the other things, not because they are easy, but because they are hard, because that goal will serve to organize and measure the best of our energies and skills, because that challenge is one that we are willing to accept, one we are unwilling to postpone, and one which we intend to win.[4]

Kennedy was, in 1962, adopting a national growth mindset. The United States was to take on the challenge of going to the moon because it was difficult, and that difficulty itself would ensure that the nation made progress at a more rapid rate than if it had taken an easier path. It was a vision which looked beyond potential, beyond what even seemed possible, to another world. Tragically, Kennedy himself was not to live to see the realisation of that vision, but it remains one of humanity's crowning achievements.

It is this spirit of ambition, and of taking on the seemingly impossible challenge, that led Google to brand their semi-secret research and development facility, X, "a moonshot factory."[5] Founded in 2010, the group aims to solve big problems by harnessing radical solutions with ground-breaking technology. They are working on artificial intelligence, self-driving cars, and balloon-powered internet access, as well as pioneering wearable technology with Glass and Google Watch. The thinking in common behind the actual moonshot, and the moonshot thinking which sits behind X, is in seeing a problem that we don't know how to solve – yet – but taking it on anyway. Part of this attitude is to accept inevitable failures along the way but keep the ultimate goal intact. This is the growth mindset and Angela Duckworth's grit writ large in corporate or national culture. It is an inspiring and ambitious message and one which I think worthy of consideration as part of a school culture.

"Attitude determines altitude" has been a fundamental message for building a growth mindset in the schools I have worked in. It captures the essence of the idea that the responsibility for progress, achievement, and performance rests with the learner and that it is their disposition and behaviour which will influence their success over and above the natural abilities that they are bringing to the table. As a banner heading, I think it sums up the message for students, staff, and families perfectly. However, as with any broad-brush statement, it runs the risk of being a platitude or an excuse without detail behind it.

One of the major projects during the first year of the growth mindset ethos at Chew Valley School was the development of an attitude scale for students. We recognised early on that we wanted students to adapt their behaviour in order to develop a growth mindset, and simply telling them to "try harder" was not going to be effective. We had already been doing that for a long time! We needed to provide specific, detailed feedback to students about particular behaviours which they needed to work on and improve in order to develop their attitude towards a growth mindset approach. At the same time, it was important for us to measure the impact of this work. Although we all agreed that students who improved their attitudes to learning would achieve better and make more progress, this was not founded on evidence. We wanted to be sure that this was the case. Did a student's attitude genuinely determine their altitude?

We approached the task with considerable caution. In a 2015 article, Angela Duckworth and David Scott Yeager[6] conclude that the kinds of measures used by Duckworth, Dweck, Mischel, and others in their research studies were not necessarily suitable for educational use. They were very concerned that in the well-intentioned urge to implement character education or the development of what they called "non-cognitive skills" – including growth mindset, grit, and self-control – schools were trying to run before they could walk.[7] The grit scale or the growth mindset questionnaires were designed to measure grittiness or growth mindset beliefs for the purpose of research studies. Schools – including ours – were trying to use them to evaluate the impact of interventions designed to develop growth mindsets or grit. There were even suggestions that schools were planning the hiring, firing, and promotion of teaching staff based on their performance in growth mindset questionnaires.[8] Duckworth and Yeager point out the many flaws and inconsistencies that can arise from self-report and teacher-report questionnaires, stemming from biases and competing motivations in completion as well as difficulties in interpretation. The only way in which such measures might have some secure effectiveness, they conclude, would be in practice improvement.

Research such as this is worthy of note – especially when it is conducted by someone like Angela Duckworth, who has devoted much of her career to promoting the importance of non-cognitive skills such as the growth mindset and, especially, grit. Clearly there is concern on her part that the research, so painstakingly conducted, was being misapplied in educational contexts. There is no doubt that we ourselves have been guilty of this, measuring students' mindsets at the start of the year and then again at the end of the year to evaluate the impact of the interventions we had put in place. A fruitless exercise, it seems, designed to tell us only what we wanted to hear.

So, embarking on the design of an attitude scale of our own, it was important to clarify the purpose. This was not a scale that we could – or would – use to evaluate the impact of specific interventions. It would not be valid to use it for within-school comparisons of teachers, students, or groups. The purpose of designing an attitude scale was, first, to be explicit with all teachers, students, and families about the attitudes and behaviours that we valued as an institution. Our attitude scale was to be a public statement of intent in relation to the things we wanted to see in our classrooms. Second, the scale was to be used with individual students to set targets and themes for them to work on over set periods of time, to demonstrate improvement through practice. Even given the potential inconsistencies in teacher-report and self-report questionnaires identified in Duckworth and Yeager's study, this felt like a vital piece in the jigsaw of developing a growth mindset school. It would also allow us to engage fully with the aspects of character and attitude that contributed to effective learning and which we would seek to prioritise as a school in our work with young people and their families.

The vehicle for providing this sort of feedback already existed at Chew Valley in the shape of the reports provided for students and their families three times a year. The reports already contained a set of "attitude grades" which saw students assessed as Very Good (V), Good (G), Satisfactory (S), or Unsatisfactory (U) in four areas: Behaviour, Classwork, Homework, and Organisation. This system was ripe for an overhaul. In the first instance, the grades themselves were unclear. Teachers were using the grade "Satisfactory" in the Ofsted-influenced educational sense of the word, where "satisfactory" means "unsatisfactory." The term had not been updated when Ofsted adopted the grade "requires improvement" instead. Second, there was confusion and crossover between the areas of attitude that were being assessed – homework and organisation, for example, had significant overlap. Although there was guidance about what should be included in each category, there was still too much grey area. Given that we were interested in developing student attitude, we gathered pastoral and curriculum middle leaders on a sixth-month project to overhaul the system and replace it with one designed to:

1. Promote a growth mindset

2. Enable specific focus on attitudes and behaviours

3. Communicate our valued behaviours clearly between teachers, students, and families.

We needed to think carefully about the particular categories of behaviour we were looking for, how we were going to assess those behaviours, and what grading system we were going to use. Since we were starting from a blank page, we saw a great opportunity to get our approach to attitudes right.

The first thing that we did was to research attitude scales used elsewhere. We gathered examples from as many other schools as we could find, borrowing from colleagues locally and nationally, and scouring the internet for school websites which published them. There was a huge array, with a wide variety of practice on offer. It seemed that every school was grading attitude or effort in some way. The approaches ranged from "effort grades" in letter format, from A* to G, like GCSE grades, without any criteria attached, to detailed ten-point scales with a list of criteria attached to each level, including the number of behaviour points accrued, percentage attendance, and homework completion. Wherever possible, we asked schools where their attitude or effort grades had come from or how they had been generated. Many said that they had been around for years and they had always used them. A few said that a working party had sat down to write them a few years ago and they'd stuck with them. Nobody seemed to have referred to any research into motivation, attitude, or disposition in the formulation of their scales.

Our second port of call, then, was to look for the research and recognised examples. There has been a vast array of work done on effective learner behaviours, and in our group we reviewed a selection of the best-known ones we could find. Strangely, we found one of the most interesting definitions of successful learning behaviour in the work of the National Strategies and their development of the Personal Learning and Thinking Skills, or PLTS as the only-just-acronym went.

The Personal Learning and Thinking Skills were developed by the Qualifications and Curriculum Authority (QCA) as part of the new 2007 National Curriculum. They were designed to sit alongside English, Maths, and ICT as the groups of skills "essential to learning, life and work."[9] As with all of the work of the QCA and the old National Curriculum, they were removed from the internet after the election in 2010 as the newly renamed Department for Education made a virtual bonfire of the previous administration's work. Fortunately for us, they were preserved by the National Archive as part of the UK Government Web Archive, probably sitting as well in dusty lever-arch files in senior leaders' offices up and down the country to this day. To be honest, we did not relish the thought of returning to the National Strategies, which were tainted by the bloated behemoth of consultancy and straitjacketing that it had become in its later years. However, we had undertaken to be open-minded, and we were glad we did.

The PLTS framework lays out six groups of skills, setting the ambition that learners need to be: independent enquirers; creative thinkers; reflective learners; team workers; self-managers; and effective participants.[10] Each set of skills is accompanied by a focus statement laying out the range of skills and qualities involved in that set along with a series of bullet-pointed "outcome statements" which exemplify the behaviours and personal qualities involved in them. Here, for example, is the focus statement for "self-managers": "Young people organise themselves, showing personal responsibility, initiative, creativity and enterprise with a commitment to learning and self-improvement. They actively embrace change, responding positively to new priorities, coping with challenges and looking for opportunities." Self-managers, then:

- seek out challenges or new responsibilities and show flexibility when priorities change

- work towards goals, showing initiative, commitment and perseverance

- organise time and resources, prioritising actions

- anticipate, take and manage risks

- deal with competing pressures, including personal and work-related demands

- respond positively to change, seeking advice and support when needed

- manage their emotions, and build and maintain relationships.[11]

Under the surface of this set of skills was an attempt at least to codify aspects of the growth mindset into a coherent set of separate but interlocking learning behaviours. The notion of "[working] towards goals" with "commitment and perseverance" is the whole topic of Angela Duckworth's study of grit. Maybe the National Strategies weren't a waste of time after all? However, the six skill areas generated a total of thirty-seven separate bullet-pointed behaviour and personal qualities, the sheer size of which soon became unmanageable.

At the other end of the complexity scale sits the KIPP public charter school approach to character, with the simple slogan: "work hard, be nice." These four words capture very effectively the core of pretty much every school behaviour policy I've ever worked with. Given its track record of transforming outcomes for some of the nation's most disadvantaged communities, there's certainly no arguing with the effectiveness of KIPP in the United States. KIPP is cited for its transformative educational approach by Walter Mischel,[12] Malcolm Gladwell,[13] and Angela Duckworth,[14] and each of them refers to the approach the charter schools take to the development of character alongside the rigorous academic foundation.

Since the foundation of KIPP in 1994, however, founder Dave Levin has been working hard to codify the learning behaviours which sit behind "work hard, be nice." Most recently, this has been alongside Angela Duckworth herself, in the non-profit CharacterLab[15] project. CharacterLab, like the QCA, has broken down successful learning behaviour into separate categories, although the research provenance of Duckworth's work is much more explicit. The CharacterLab approach clusters character strengths into three areas: strengths of heart, strengths of mind, and strengths of will.

Strengths of heart are described as the "helping" strengths and include gratitude, purpose, interpersonal self-control, and social/emotional intelligence, helping you to relate to other people in a positive way. The CharacterLab strengths of will are grit, growth mindset, and optimism, helping you to achieve your goals – the "doing strengths." Finally, the strengths of mind, or "thinking" strengths, are curiosity, self-control in your work, and zest or vitality – an approach to life filled with excitement and energy.[16] Seven of these are now embedded in the KIPP approach to character, which prioritises zest, grit, optimism, self-control, gratitude, social intelligence, and curiosity as the character strengths which are the greatest predictors of success in later life. For this reason, KIPP schools explicitly teach these character strengths as part of their curriculum programme. You can even download a "Character Growth Card" assessment tool, with a seven-point scale attached, from the KIPP website.[17]

These were not the only examples that we found. Guy Claxton and Bill Lucas had also developed a model of "desired outcomes for education" or DOEs in 2013, many of which focused on character traits, behaviours, or attitudes to learning. They classified the DOEs as "prosocial" (those concerned with good citizenship,

Table 8.1 Desired outcomes of education (DOEs)

Prosocial DOEs	Epistemic DOEs
• Kind (not callous)	• Inquisitive (not passive)
• Generous (not greedy)	• Resilient (not easily defeated)
• Forgiving (not vindictive)	• Imaginative (not literal)
• Tolerant (not bigoted)	• Craftsmanlike (not slapdash)
• Trustworthy (not deceitful)	• Sceptical (not credulous)
• Morally brave (not apathetic)	• Collaborative (not selfish)
• Convivial (not egotistical)	• Thoughtful (not impulsive)
• Ecological (not rapacious)	• Practical (not only "academic")

Source: Claxton and Lucas (2013)

attitude, and behaviour) and "epistemic" (those concerned with "the qualities of mind of the powerful learner"[18]) (Table 8.1).

The work Claxton and Lucas were undertaking was clearly more wide-ranging than just considering attitudes to learning, exploring as they were the very purpose of education with the intention of redesigning schooling. But in doing that work, there were clearly attitudes within both their prosocial and epistemic DOEs which had significant bearing on the learning process. There again, just like the PLTS from the National Strategies and CharacterLab and KIPP's Character Growth Card, we found the growth mindset emphasised. Here it manifested as being inquisitive and resilient, characterised as being active and "not easily defeated." This is similar to KIPP's "curiosity" and "grit," or the PLTS' "self-manager" and "independent enquirers." The common threads were starting to emerge.

Further down the rabbit hole we went. In California, Dr Art Costa and his team have developed a model called "Habits of Mind."[19] Costa himself was once director of educational programmes at NASA,[20] so surely if anyone was going to be able to help us with "attitude determines altitude," it was him. Costa's work, alongside his colleague Bena Kallick, interested us not just because of the NASA connection. At his Centre for Thinking, he and his team have attempted to codify what successful learners do when encountering a problem to which they don't have the solution or a question to which they don't know the answer. Behaviour in this "struggle zone" was of critical importance to us as this was where the fixed mindset approach would be to give up, whereas the growth mindset learner would persist and take on the challenge. According to the Centre for Thinking, there are sixteen habits of mind:

1. Persisting

2. Thinking and communicating with clarity and precision

3. Managing impulsivity

4. Gathering data through all senses

5. Listening with understanding and empathy

6. Creating, imagining, innovating

7. Thinking flexibly

8. Responding with wonderment and awe

9. Thinking about thinking (metacognition)

10. Taking responsible risks

11. Striving for accuracy

12. Finding humour

13. Questioning and posing problems

14. Thinking interdependently

15. Applying past knowledge to new situations

16. Remaining open to continuous learning[21]

There was a wealth of work behind the habits of mind, all designed to improve independence and encourage learners to "unstick" themselves when faced with challenging tasks. There was clear crossover between the models we had already examined, with the self-control emphasised by KIPP and CharacterLab evident again in the third habit: managing impulsivity. In turn, we saw this in Claxton and Lucas' epistemic DOE: thoughtful (not impulsive). KIPP's optimism and zest clearly have areas of common ground with Costa's eighth and twelfth habits: responding with wonderment and awe, and finding humour. The resilience prioritised by Claxton and Lucas, and characterised as grit by Duckworth at CharacterLab, is the first of Costa's habits of mind: persisting.

However, although the areas of crossover and intersection were clear to us, there were shades of difference between them. Duckworth defines grit as "passion and perseverance for long-term goals."[22] This is a more nuanced definition than just "persisting," as it requires the definition of that goal but also the passion which accompanies a desired outcome. Persistence requires resilience, but they are not one and the same thing. Persistence is the stubborn pursuit of a course of action in the face of opposition or difficulty, whereas resilience is more about recovery after being subjected to difficulty. Although resilience is the word more often associated with growth mindset, having become something of a buzzword in education in terms of developing attitudes to learning, might persistence be the quality that we were in fact trying to cultivate?

Our research then moved, virtually, from California to Australia and the Project for Enhancing Effective Learning (or PEEL).[23] Founded in 1985, PEEL is a great example of a grass-roots teacher movement, similar to the TeachMeets that have swept across the United Kingdom over recent years. PEEL was set up by a group of teachers and academics, unfunded, outside any national or state initiative, to try and tackle the problem of passive, dependent learners. As a group, they sought to identify teaching practice which would develop students' use of more responsive, responsible, active, independent, and metacognitive approaches. We were not blind to the irony of the fact that we were pursuing the same quest thirty years later, with the problem still unresolved on a systemic scale.

PEEL has generated a wealth of interesting material, but for our purposes we were most interested in their list of good learning behaviours:

1. Checks personal comprehension for instruction and material. Requests further information if needed. Tells the teacher what they don't understand.

2. Seeks reasons for aspects of the work at hand.

3. Plans a general strategy before starting.

4. Anticipates and predicts possible outcomes.

5. Checks teacher's work for errors; offers corrections.

6. Offers or seeks links between: different activities and ideas, different topics or subjects, schoolwork and personal life.

7. Searches for weaknesses in their own understandings; checks the consistency of their explanations across different situations.

8. Suggests new activities and alternative procedures.

9. Challenges the text or an answer the teacher sanctions as correct.

10. Offers ideas, new insights and alternative explanations.

11. Justifies opinions.

12. Reacts and refers to comments of other students.[24]

Interestingly, this was the most controversial of all the taxonomies we identified in our research. In discussion of these learning behaviours, we tried to visualise a full class of thirty Year 9 students, all seeking to challenge the answer the teacher had sanctioned as correct, suggesting alternative activities that they would rather be doing, and continually asking why they were doing this work in the first place (behaviour 2). In our planning, we were able to anticipate and predict the possible outcomes of adopting such a strategy, and we weren't thrilled at the prospect of the potential unintended consequences of the approach. Nevertheless, we could see that the PEEL learning behaviours were a direct response to passive, uninvolved, and uninterested learners and that it would work as an antidote to this issue. There was a clear link to the "sceptical (not credulous)" DOE identified by Claxton and Lucas, and behaviours 1 and 7 crossed over into the metacognitive habit advocated by Art Costa. Despite our reservations, there were elements within PEEL's list of behaviours that were of value to us.

In total, we gathered twenty-three separate areas from our school and research sweep that we felt could be used for assessing students' attitudes. These were:

1. Curiosity
2. Teamwork
3. Purpose
4. Gratitude
5. Organisation
6. Homework
7. Grit
8. Independent enquiry
9. Self-discipline
10. Creative thinking
11. Self-management
12. Resilience
13. Zest
14. Persistence
15. Classwork
16. Self-control
17. Reflection
18. Social-emotional intelligence
19. Response to feedback
20. Independence
21. Metacognition
22. Participation
23. Optimism

Some were clearly more problematic than others. In one example, we discarded the idea of sending home a grade for a student's "social-emotional intelligence" as one that could too easily be interpreted as an assessment of a student's natural ability, rather than their behaviour. Similarly, "homework" and "classwork," although common across schools in our sample (and in our existing system), were not in and of themselves attitudes or behaviours, but rather outcomes from attitudes and behaviours. The sixteen habits of mind and twelve learning behaviours we had found were useful scales, but they were too large in scale to be manageable in a reporting system. The same was true of our experiences with the personal, learning, and thinking skills. They were recent enough innovations for us to remember students with individual PLTS portfolios evidencing their achievements against the thirty-seven separate outcome statements – or, worse, teachers having to do the same, with a class of thirty generating over a thousand tick boxes in one fell swoop. There was much work to do in refining our trawl of potential student attitude areas into a manageable system that could be implemented with purpose and impact.

How do you describe attitudes?

Once we'd gathered all of these different ways of breaking down student attitudes, we set about selecting, synthesising, and collating to create the rubric that we wanted for our school, and working out which language we should use to describe it. As explained earlier, we were looking to replace a system where attitudes were described as Very Good (V), Good (G), Satisfactory (S), and Unsatisfactory (U), with all the confusion inherent in the contrast between the educational establishment's understanding of "satisfactory" (a noun meaning "not good enough") and the understanding of students, families, and the community at large (where it is a noun meaning "good enough").

Alongside the evidence we had gathered for taxonomies describing student effort in schools, we had also gathered their grading systems. The most common were numerical scales, ranging from four-point to ten-point scales, followed closely by graded scales reflecting GCSE grades with A* to G awarded for effort alongside achievement, attainment, or performance grades. Although we were unhappy with our V-G-S-U system, we did feel that a descriptor system was more helpful than a graded system with either numbers or letters, as it communicated an expectation about students' approaches to learning as well as assessing them.

Again, we cast the net wide to look for examples of practice across the country and abroad. James Webber, our Head of Computing, conducted extensive research into US effort rubrics, uncovering examples including:

- Exceptional, Accomplished, Developing, Beginning

- Awesome, Admirable, Acceptable, Attempted[25]

- Distinguished, Proficient, Apprentice, Amateur

- Always, Sometimes, Not Yet

- Master, Veteran, Apprentice, Novice

- Excellent, Good, Fair, Weak

- Exemplary, Proficient, Marginal, Unacceptable

- Exemplary, Consistent, Inconsistent, Poor

We even toyed with J. K. Rowling's achievement scale from the Harry Potter books, but decided that Outstanding, Exceeds Expectations, Acceptable, Poor, Dreadful, and Troll would not be fit for purpose in our muggle context (as well as being discriminatory against trolls).

In these cases, although some rubrics were clearly applied to effort, there was considerable crossover with academic achievement in the scales. We wanted to ensure that there was a clear distinction between feedback on a student's attitude and their attainment.

John Tomsett, who had been so influential from the outset on our approach to growth mindset schooling, had also wrestled with the challenge of finding accurate terminology to describe students' effort.[26] At his school, they settled on a four-point scale of Excellent, Good, Insufficient, and Poor. In particular, the use of "insufficient" was proving controversial, and he sought advice from his staff and his blog's readers. There were over seventy responses offering support, or alternatives, to the descriptors he was wrestling with.

What was self-evident was the fact that terminology was a complex and difficult area, and there was never going to be a single "right answer" to this work. We evaluated each option in turn, picking over strengths and weaknesses in their application to our own school. We spent a long time thinking about "always, sometimes, not yet," as that rubric seemed to us to capture most accurately the idea of a growth mindset approach.[27] Like John Tomsett, we wrestled with the tension between honesty and brutality in the use of "insufficient." We rejected "requires improvement" not because it was unfit for purpose but simply because it was tainted for us with overtones of external accountability through its use in Ofsted inspections.

Following a joint meeting of pastoral and curriculum middle leaders to agree the framework, it fell to our school's teaching and learning middle leadership group to knock the final document into shape for trials in the first year and refinement over time. In the end we designed the grid in Table 8.2 (pages 92–93).

Our aim in creating the grid was to try to describe observable behaviours which students demonstrated in class. Teachers who observed these behaviours would then be able to grade them accordingly. We used those grades to provide an attitude percentage score at each monitoring point by assigning values to each of the attitudes in our assessment system: three points for each Excellent, two for each Good, one for each Insufficient, and zero for a Poor. By using a formula to add the total and divide by the maximum possible total, we were able to create a percentage score which would allow simple tracking of improvement or decline in attitude over time. This would then trigger praise and reward or intervention and discussion. But because it's split into four areas, tutors and teachers could mine the data to see specifically where changes in attitudes occurred – an improvement in response to feedback, for example, or an improvement in attitude in one particular subject which affected the total. This data-driven approach to attitudes to learning gave teachers and tutors a way in to exploring the attitudes with students, praising them, for example, for a rise of 6 per cent since the last time their attitude was assessed and setting them targets for their improvements.

Most important was explicit teaching of the attitude expectations to students. We used an off-timetable session for this, so the whole school worked on the new attitude grades together. Students self-assessed against the criteria and set targets for improvement, as well as discussing what exactly it would look like in the classroom to display the attitudes in the "excellent" column. This was accompanied by teachers working to create opportunities in lessons to make explicit to the students the attitudes they expected to see. Teachers were encouraged to set up tasks in the classroom with specific reference to the new attitude grid. I saw a great example in an English lesson I observed where the teacher set up the task – reading a challenging non-fiction text and inferring the author's tone – as "an opportunity to respond positively to a challenge" and one which would require them to persevere. This was then reinforced with praise for those students who demonstrated those behaviours while struggling with the difficulty of the task. It was a great way of ensuring students could see the application of attitudes in a subject-specific context.

We also provided information for parents and families through letters, including the table on the reports, and face-to-face at information evenings. It was vital to us that families understood why we were changing what we were doing, and why we believed that attitudes to learning mattered so much, so they could support us in developing the best possible approaches to study.

Over time, we saw some interesting impacts from our work using the behaviour for learning grid. First, it ensured the recognition of those students sometimes referred to as "the forgotten middle." These students, who achieve well and never cause any trouble, can often be missed. They're not the highest academic attainers so they rarely make it to the top of an attainment assessment spreadsheet. They don't rack up behaviour points so they don't register on intervention lists for pastoral teams. They achieve at or close to their targets so they don't get flagged for special attention from curriculum teams. They don't get in trouble – but they don't get the plaudits either. What the explicit tracking of attitudes started to do was to highlight those students by separating their attitudes from their attainment grades. It showed those students who were improving their attitudes over time, highlighting the strides they had made. It identified those students whose attitudes were consistently good over time and allowed us to make praise calls home to recognise this.

It also started to have an impact on the students themselves. Over the course of a year, the average attitude score in Year 11, for example, showed an upward trend. The students themselves were improving their attitudes. Not all of them of course – but we had data to help us intervene with those who were getting worse. But there were also spectacular successes with students who saw where they stood in relation to their peers and decided that they were going to do something about it. The key to this was that we were clear, at all times, that your attitude – the way you behave towards your learning – is something that you can control. Whilst you might not be able to have an effect on your natural ability in a subject, whatever your genes predispose you to be able to do, all bar a very tiny minority of children with very specific special educational needs are able to control their behaviour in

Table 8.2 Attitude to learning grid from Chew Valley School

	Behaviour for Learning			
	Excellent	**Good**	**Insufficient**	**Poor**
Conduct Guidance	• L3 rewards given • Positive conduct score	• May have L3 rewards • Positive conduct score	• L2 sanctions applied	• L2 or 3 sanctions applied • Negative conduct score
Attitude to learning	• Excellent focus • Rarely off-task • Seeks challenge • Perseveres • Asks questions to extend thinking • Approaches learning with active interest	• Good focus • Responds positively to challenging activities • Completes all work set to good standard • Answers questions • Connects ideas	• Poor focus • Avoids challenging tasks • Gives up easily • Passive in the classroom • Does as little as possible	• Shows little focus • Disrupts the classroom • Work often incomplete or inadequate
Response to feedback	• Invites feedback • Responds positively to praise and critique • Learns from setbacks and mistakes • Reviews own progress, acting on the outcomes	• Shows a desire to improve • Takes action based on feedback • Shows progress over time	• Sometimes attempts to act on feedback • Needs close direction to rectify errors or learn from mistakes	• Does not attempt to act on feedback • Responds negatively to praise or critique

Independent study			
• Starts learning readily • Seeks own solutions to problems • Asks questions • Organises time effectively • Meets all deadlines	• Shows good application • Can find solutions to problems • Seeks help when needed • Organises time well • Meets deadlines	• Requires close supervision to attempt tasks • Gives up easily • Misses some deadlines	• Normally requires pressure to attempt learning tasks • Does not engage unless closely monitored • May refuse support • Misses most deadlines

Behaviour			
• Seeks solutions to difficulties • Sets an example • Takes responsibility • Acts as an advocate for views and beliefs that may differ from their own	• Follows all instructions • Shows kindness, consideration and respect • Listens carefully • Understands views of others	• Requires supervision to ensure instructions are followed • May distract others • May be off-task • Struggles to understand the views of others	• Does not listen • Distracts others • Disrupts the classroom or school environment

Chew Valley School

learning. By talking about this explicitly and requiring students to act on it, we saw significant improvements in attitude scores over time, in some cases by as much as 15 per cent.

The final piece of the jigsaw came when we matched students' GCSE outcomes with their attitudes to learning. This was a moment of truth. Having pinned our approach on the idea that students' attitudes determined their altitudes, would this be borne out by the data?

Fortunately, the answer was yes. Admittedly, the sample size was small – just one year group within our school – and the attitude scale we were using was still subjective, even though we had tried to link it wherever possible to observable student behaviours. But on the evidence we had, there was a positive correlation between the attitude to learning a student showed through the course of Year 11 and the average points score they achieved in their GCSEs. There would need to be more robust studies done to replicate this data, but it was enough for us to stand in front of the new Year 11 the following September and show them the graph and demonstrate that if they had a positive attitude, as measured on the behaviour for learning scale, they would be more likely to score a good set of GCSE results.

There were outliers in the data, of course. One student with a lovely attitude and a positive approach throughout the year scored relatively low on the GCSE average points score. This student's "dot" sits way above the trend line and is due, in part, to the significant learning difficulties they had been dealing with. Conversely, there were outliers well below the line – students with pretty terrible attitudes to learning who still scored an impressive set of GCSE results. These students – the ones who "got away with it" at GCSE – were particularly frustrating, but we couldn't help wondering if they had done that well with a poor attitude to learning, how well could they have done if they had improved their attitude? And we suspected – rightly – that they could no longer get away with it at A-level and that attitudes would either change or grades dip.

Since that first trial, we have continued to work on and review our scales and to implement the approach. In the latest version of the attitude scale in use at Churchill Academy & Sixth Form, the "categories" of behaviour have been removed, so teachers only need to enter one grade, not four, when they are called on for assessments.

You can see from Table 8.3 that in a new context, we have tweaked and revised the descriptors and some of the attitudes again. I'm sure we will continue to do so, because I'm certain we haven't got it right – yet. But the approach, and the direct engagement with students and their families over the attitudes and behaviours which are indicative of a growth mindset, is vital to the process. I would encourage you to have the conversation in your own school. What does great learning behaviour look like? And what can we do to make sure it happens?

Table 8.3 Attitude to learning grid from Churchill Academy & Sixth Form

Highly Motivated	Engaged	Passive	Disengaged
• Excellent focus	• Good focus	• Not always focused	• Shows little focus
• Seeks challenge	• Responds positively to challenging activities	• Avoids challenging tasks	• Work often incomplete or inadequate
• Perseveres			
• Asks questions to extend thinking		• Not always working hard	• Does not attempt to act on feedback
• Approaches learning with active interest	• Completes all work set to good standard	• Sometimes attempts to act on feedback	• Responds negatively to praise or critique
• Invites feedback	• Answers questions		
• Responds positively to praise and critique	• Connects ideas	• Requires close supervision to ensure tasks are attempted and instructions followed	• Normally needs pressure to attempt learning tasks
• Learns from setbacks and mistakes	• Shows a desire to improve		
	• Takes action based on feedback		• Does not engage unless closely monitored
• Reviews own progress, acting on the outcomes	• Shows good application	• Misses some deadlines	• May refuse support
• Starts learning readily	• Can find solutions to problems	• May distract others	• Misses most deadlines
• Seeks own solutions to problems	• Seeks help when needed	• May be off-task	• Does not listen
	• Organises time well	• May be unprepared for lessons	• Distracts others
• Asks questions	• Follows all instructions	• Relies on others to do the work	• Disrupts the classroom or school environment
• Organises time effectively			
• Sets an example	• Shows kindness, consideration and respect	• Shows a lack of effort at times	• Rarely prepared for lessons
• Takes responsibility	• Listens carefully		

Notes

1 NASA, *Superstars of Spaceflight*.
2 Pearsall, *The Concise Oxford Dictionary*.
3 National Visionary Leadership Project, "Katherine Johnson."
4 Kennedy, "John F. Kennedy moon speech."
5 X, "What we do."

6 Duckworth & Yeager, "Measurement matters."

7 Ibid.

8 "Adapting and using these measures to decide . . . how to promote or hire or fire teachers, principals, or staff . . . [is not] what the measures were developed for" (Yeager, "Researchers urge caution in using measures of students' 'non-cognitive' skills").

9 Qualifications and Curriculum Authority, "Personal learning and thinking skills."

10 Ibid.

11 Ibid.

12 Mischel, *The Marshmallow Test.*

13 Gladwell, *Outliers.*

14 Duckworth, *Grit.*

15 CharacterLab, "Why does CharacterLab exist?"

16 We used the CharacterLab strengths to help formulate the values we hold at Churchill Academy & Sixth Form: Kindness (strength of heart), Curiosity (strength of mind), and Determination (strength of will).

17 KIPP, "Focus on character."

18 Claxton & Lucas, *What Kind of Teaching for What Kind of Learning?*, page 9.

19 Costa & Kallick, *Habits of Mind Across the Curriculum.*

20 Costa's biography is listed by the ASCD: www.ascd.org/Publications/ascd-authors/art-costa.aspx

21 The Art Costa Centre for Thinking, "What is habits of mind."

22 Duckworth, op. cit.

23 PEEL, "Good learning behaviours."

24 Ibid.

25 From a Californian school setting (http://score.rims.k12.ca.us/activity/world_history_fair/pages/eval.html)

26 Tomsett, "This much I know about using accurate terminology to describe students' effort."

27 The use of the grade "not yet" is promoted by Jo Boaler and others in their work to promote a growth mindset in students (https://www.mindsetkit.org/practices/TMvw JYx4zTictvnb).

Bibliography

CharacterLab. (2016, 11 December). Why does CharacterLab exist?. Retrieved 14 January, 2017, from *CharacterLab*: https://characterlab.org/about

Claxton, G., & Lucas, B. (2013). *What Kind of Teaching for What Kind of Learning? Redesigning Schooling.* London: SSAT.

Costa, A. L., & Kallick, B. (2009). *Habits of Mind Across the Curriculum.* Alexandria, VA: ASCD.

Duckworth, A. (2016). *Grit.* London: Vermilion.

Duckworth, A. L., & Yeager, D. S. (2015, 1 May). Measurement matters: Assessing personal qualities other than cognitive ability for educational purposes. *Educational Researcher,* *44*(4), 237–251.

Gladwell, M. (2009). *Outliers.* London: Penguin.

Kennedy, J. (1962, 12 September). John F. Kennedy moon speech – Rice Stadium. Retrieved 8 January 2017, from *Space Movies Cinema*: https://er.jsc.nasa.gov/seh/ricetalk.htm

KIPP. (2016). Focus on character. Retrieved 14 January, 2017, from *KIPP*: www.kipp.org/approach/character/

Mischel, W. (2015). *The Marshmallow Test.* London: Transworld Publishers.

NASA. (1996). *Superstars of Spaceflight.* Oberlin, OH: NASA.

National Visionary Leadership Project. (2005). Katherine Johnson: National visionary. Retrieved 8 January, 2017, from *National Visionary Leadership Project*: www.visionary project.org/johnsonkatherine/

Pearsall, J. (1999). *The Concise Oxford Dictionary* (10th edition). Oxford: Oxford University Press.

PEEL. (2009). Good learning behaviours. Retrieved 14 January, 2017, from *Project for Enhancing Effective Learning*: www.peelweb.org/index.cfm?resource=good%20behaviours

Qualifications and Curriculum Authority. (2011, 15 February). Personal learning and thinking skills. Retrieved 14 January, 2017, from *The National Archives*: http://webarchive.natio nalarchives.gov.uk/20110223175304/http:/curriculum.qcda.gov.uk/key-stages-3-and-4/ skills/personal-learning-and-thinking-skills/index.aspx

Stix, A. (1996, 1 November). Creating rubrics through negotiable contracting and assessment. *National Middle School Conference.* Baltimore, MD: OERI.

The Art Costa Centre for Thinking. (2004, 30 November). What is habits of mind. Retrieved 14 January, 2017, from *The Art Costa Centre for Thinking*: www.artcostacentre.com/html/ habits.htm

Tomsett, J. (2014, 28 June). This much I know about using accurate terminology to describe students' effort. Retrieved 15 January, 2017, from John Tomsett's blog: https://johntom sett.com/2014/06/28/this-much-i-know-aboutaccurate-terminology-to-describe-stu dents-effort/

X. (2010). What we do. Retrieved 8 January, 2017, from *X*: https://x.company/about

Yeager, D. (2015, 13 May). Researchers urge caution in using measures of students' "non-cognitive" skills. Retrieved 14 January, 2017, from *American Educational Research Association*: www.aera.net/Newsroom/News-Releases-and-Statements/Researchers-Urge-Caution-in-Using-Measures-of-Students-Non-Cognitive-Skills-for-Teacher-Evaluation-School-Accountability-or-Student-Diagnosis

9 Language and interaction in a growth mindset school

One of Dweck's most widely shared and celebrated findings is that mindsets can be influenced by the language used by teachers and other adults in schools. In the studies she completed on the effect of praise on student motivation and achievement, for example, she found that changing the way in which students were praised had significant impacts not only on their motivation and willingness to take on a challenge, but also on their attainment outcomes on further assessment. Praising children for their intelligence – "wow, you must be *smart* at this" – switched them off to learning and meant that they did less well on IQ-style assessments later in the study, whereas praising them for the process – "wow, you must have *tried* really hard" – saw them persist longer with really difficult problems and actually improve their outcomes on future assessments. Dweck and others have also found, in other studies,[1] that mothers' praise to their babies, between 1 and 3 years old, had significant impact on the children's mindsets and motivational frameworks five years later.

Research like this shows the impact that praise can have on the children we teach in school. The language that we use is the transmission system for the values we hold, and the way we speak about motivation, achievement, attainment, strategy, and process will influence the way that those elements of education are perceived by the learners in the school. Therefore, if we constantly praise high achievement but do not link that high achievement to the strategy, process, and effort by which it was reached, we risk undermining motivation among other students to see similar feats as being within their own grasp. Or, to put it another way, if we focus all of our language and interaction with the students in our schools on the strategies, processes, and effort they are using to tackle and solve problems, improve their attainment, and make progress, we are showing that we value this approach and we are more likely to establish a growth mindset culture.

How, then, do we change and develop the language and interaction in our schools so that the process of learning is valued over the achievement and natural ability that students bring to the tasks they are tackling? The first way that I have worked on this with teachers in the schools where I have launched a growth mindset culture is to explore the preconceptions and messages which underpin the language that we use in the classroom. The first step is understanding that language along the lines of "you must be really smart at this" has a detrimental impact, whilst saying "you must have tried really hard" has a positive one. But the next is to ask staff within the school to think about phrases and interactions within schools which are part of our lexicon but also contain similar underlying messages. What else do we say in our classrooms, our marking, our written reports, our verbal feedback, and our interactions with students and their families which could also be developing growth or fixed mindsets?

Implementing growth mindset language in schools

I often start the discussions with a phrase from a written school report. As Deputy Headteacher, it was my role to proofread and check the written reports produced by teachers, making sure that the correct student names were included in the comments and that the messages were clear, accurate, and helpful. When first thinking about growth mindset, I came across a report which began with the following comment: "You are a bright girl, Abigail, and you are clearly a gifted historian." In fact, she wasn't called Abigail and it wasn't a history report, but the example still stands. I use this comment to start discussions with staff in school. The teacher is impressed with Abigail; she is doing well in her history; the intention is to praise. But what message does this kind of praise give about the need for hard work, effort, and resilience if that achievement in history is going to continue? It implies that Abigail, with her intelligence and natural ability "gifted" from above, should find history easy. This kind of feedback perpetuates the myth that if you have talent, you shouldn't need effort – in Dweck's view, one of the worst beliefs you can have. What, then, could the teacher have said instead?

The discussion springing up from this question is the most useful starting point for staff to engage with the connection between language and mindset. Thinking about how we phrase our commentary so that it is designed for maximum positive impact on learning is the ultimate goal. What alternatives might you find to these praise statements?

- You are a talented student.

- You learn quickly.

- You find learning easy.

- You have a natural gift.

- You are a brilliant student.

- You did really well.

- You got that with no problem – well done!

But why shouldn't we praise students for success? Why is it wrong to say "you did really well"? Of course, it isn't "wrong" to say this, but it is worth considering what we are implying and how we follow it up in the next sentence. In isolation, "you did really well" is a neutral statement as it doesn't carry particular values. However, a student more inclined towards fixed mindset thinking is likely to attribute that success to their own natural ability, whereas a student more inclined towards growth mindset thinking is more likely to attribute it to the process, effort, and strategies they used to achieve that success. As a teacher, using the phrase in isolation means we miss an opportunity to reinforce that growth mindset thinking or redirect the fixed mindset thinking, nudging the beliefs that learners hold towards the connection between effort and outcome.

Following this work with staff on alternatives to common phrases in schools, we came up with the following options:

- Instead of "you are a talented student," try "you show a keen interest in this subject."

- Instead of "you learn quickly," try "you find good solutions to problems and you are keen to respond to tasks."

- Instead of "you find learning easy," try "you put in the effort so that you can learn."

- Instead of "you have a natural gift," try "you put lots of effort into showing what you know about the subject, and you're always keen to discover more."

- Instead of "you are a brilliant student," try "you have demonstrated excellent skill in applying what you have learned," or even "you have grasped some complex ideas and you are able to articulate them really skilfully."

- Instead of "you did really well," try "you did really well because you listened carefully, maintained your focus on the task, and used the resources around you skilfully."

- And finally, instead of "you got that with no problem – well done!" why not try "I'm sorry that you're finding this too easy. Don't worry – next time we'll do something harder which you can learn from!"

The final example shows something interesting and important about these praise phrases, connected to the arguments I put forward in Chapter 7. If students are getting everything right, they may well be naturally talented and excellent students – but are you challenging them enough as a teacher? If they are getting everything right, the chances are they are just showing you what they already know and what they can already do. They are, most likely, still in their comfort zone. If we want them to learn, we need to move them forward to the point where they are making mistakes and struggling – and this is the point where it is vital that praise comes. "Well done for struggling with that!" or "that was really tough, wasn't it? That's where the learning happens."

Modelling a growth mindset

Changing the language used in schools is one thing, and this is definitely an important first step. However, recent research[2] has shown that simply saying the right things, though helpful, may not be enough on its own to develop a growth mindset culture. There's a famous truism that 93 per cent of our communication is non-verbal.[3] Whilst this figure is certainly dubious, it is true that what we do, as much as what we say, matters. For example, no matter how much we say we have a growth mindset and that we embrace struggle and difficulty, no matter how much we emphasise that mistakes are an important part of the learning process, and no matter how many posters of "famous failures" we have on our classroom walls, when a student in our class *actually fails*, we are disappointed. In that moment when we hear the incorrect answer, or when we're reading the student's work with them and realising that they've got it wrong, we might be able to catch ourselves and get the right growth mindset response out verbally – "okay, Chloe, you haven't got this yet." But in that intake of breath, the flicker of our eyes, or the grimace that shadows across our face, Chloe is already deflated.

Despite our best intentions, defaulting to a fixed mindset appears to be a frequent occurrence. Angela Duckworth acknowledges that even in research where she is working alongside Carol Dweck and Marty Seligman, they default to a fixed mindset:

> All of us know how we'd *like* to react when, say, someone we're supervising brings us work that falls short of expectations.
> [. . .] But we're human. . . . We show our impatience. In judging the person's abilities, we allow a flicker of doubt to distract us momentarily from the more important task of what they could do next to improve.[4]

When this happens – and it seems inevitable that it will – it's worth unpacking the moment and working to understand it. Because failure does hurt and it is disappointing, there shouldn't be any problem with expressing this disappointment verbally or non-verbally, then looking for solutions. The issue arises when there is a mismatch between what our words are saying and what our body language is communicating. When we're saying that mistakes are a natural part of learning, but our body language is telling the students something else, our students are smart enough to pick up on it.

The same is also true of our attitudes to high achievement, modelling, and demonstration. Our attitudes as teachers to the top-performing students in our classes and schools is watched keenly and closely by others and can trigger a child's highly developed sense of fairness (or the lack of it). Do we accord special privileges in our schools to the top-performing students? Are they the ones who become monitors, who are trusted to run errands, who give out the books, who get badges and merits? And are those privileges always earned as a result of effort and attitude, or are they given simply on the grounds that the students are high performers? Do we send the brightest girl in our class to run the errand because we know she'll catch up with the work *without having to try too hard*? And what does this attitude communicate about the value we place on hard work and effort? We run the risk, in scenarios like this, of having our actions undermine our words.

In short, if we are to implement a growth mindset ethos, then changing our language is just the start. As teachers and leaders, we need to genuinely adopt a growth mindset approach in our classrooms, not just change the way we talk to students about their approach and about their work. Our actions, the behaviours and attitudes we value and reward, need to support those words or the words themselves will be rendered meaningless. If we react to mistakes as though they are a problem and if we reward high achievement even if it isn't linked to effort, this runs counter to the ethos we are trying to create. Instead, we really need to believe that mistakes help us learn, and we should only reward high achievement when it demonstrates progress linked to effort and attitude. We also reserve the right, of course, to express our disappointment and frustration when students don't even try!

A 2014 study by David Yeager, Geoffrey Cohen, and colleagues shows the impact that an emphasis on the expectations that we have of all our students could have when linked to the unconditional positive regard and support that we provide.[5] In their study, teachers provided written feedback on student essays in the margins and at the end, with suggestions for improvement. The researchers intercepted the essays and added a Post-it note to each one. Half of the essays had a Post-it note which read: "I'm giving you these comments because I have very high expectations and I know that you can reach them." The other half had identical Post-it notes with the message: "I'm giving you these comments so that you'll have feedback on your paper." Neither the students nor their teachers knew that there were different messages on the Post-it notes, as the essays were handed back in opaque folders. The first Post-it contained an important message about high expectations, positive regard, and the belief in incremental development that underpins a growth mindset ethos. The second is a carefully worded neutral message designed to act as a "placebo" in the experiment.

All students were given the opportunity to revise their essays and hand in an improved version the following week. About 40 per cent of students who had received the "placebo" feedback did so, but 80 per cent of students who had received the positive regard feedback – double the percentage who had the placebo – chose to revise their work. Again, as with Dweck's experiments with process praise, thoughtfully adjusting the message teachers communicate had a demonstrable impact on student behaviours and outcomes. Walking the talk, practising what we preach, actions speaking louder than words – whatever we call it – if we *say* we believe in students' capacity to learn and grow, we have to *show* that we believe it too. Our every communication needs to be laced with the expectation that students will try, because we care about them and their future.

The curse of "gifted and talented"

I've never liked the term "gifted and talented." I remember a time when we had to arbitrarily identify the top 10 per cent of students in each subject and log them as our "gifted and talented cohort" – even when they patently weren't! What Dweck's research shows is that the term itself conveys fixed mindset thinking and runs the risk of turning children off to learning. If you are told that you are a "gifted" mathematician, the implication is that you are naturally good at maths. This carries with it the idea that because you are so brilliant, you should find maths easy and, therefore, shouldn't really need to try. But what then happens when you run up against a difficult maths problem – perhaps when you step up to A-level, or when you encounter a Further Maths question? If you've always been told you're brilliant and you've always found it easy, you are unprepared to deal with the situation when it gets tough. You lack the strategies to cope with difficulty. Suddenly, your self-image as "brilliant mathematician" is in jeopardy because here is a bit of maths that you are struggling with and that you don't know how to do. This is the risk that "gifted and talented" label runs.

So what can we use as an alternative? We need to identify and monitor those at the very top end to ensure they are receiving sufficient stretch and challenge. If they aren't gifted and talented, what are they? In a growth mindset school, we talk about "high-attaining students." These students have achieved excellent outcomes in their assessments and have demonstrated high attainment. However, that high attainment is not some kind of inalienable right or "gift" – it is the result of their hard work, effort, and determination. If they stop applying that hard work, effort, and determination, there is every chance that they will cease to be a high-attaining student. The message we are sending with this label is that it is the process and the strategies that the children use that allow them to be high attaining, not their natural abilities.

Setting goals, or how to get an A: the best homework I've ever set

One way that I have found of engaging students with the idea of growth mindset is through a self-reflective homework inspired by Benjamin Zander. At the start of the year, conductor and teacher Zander gives all the students in his legendary musical interpretation class at the Boston Conservatory an A. There is only one condition to this grade. Within the first two weeks of the year, the students must write him a letter. He explains,

> the letter must be dated the following May, when the class ends. The letter must begin with these words: "Dear Mr Zander, I got my A because. . . ." Then they have to write a letter describing who they will have become by the following May to justify this extraordinary grade . . . then the person

that I teach is the person that they describe in their letter. You see, I only take A students.[6]

When I heard this story, told in Zander's flamboyant style, I was intrigued. It seemed to have a lot in common with the approaches advocated by Walter Mischel to use the "hot" and "cool" systems in the brain and those suggested by Angela Duckworth in order to create a higher-level goal. By visualising a future self, the students create a concrete reality to aim for. By describing the person that they will have become in order to deserve the A grade, they automatically identify the behaviours, approaches, attitudes, and strategies they will need to adopt to overcome the self-identified weaknesses in their musicianship and to build on their strengths. I set about adapting Zander's model for use in my own classroom.

Whilst I applaud Zander's egalitarian approach to grading (he does not amend the grades throughout the year, assuming that every student will get the A they have set themselves – a luxury perhaps of teaching in an exclusive selective conservatory for exceptional musicians), this was not an aspect I felt comfortable adopting with my GCSE English class at the start of Year 10. I was not confident that they would all get an A. However, I did believe that they were all *capable* of getting an A, and I was absolutely confident that the curriculum I had planned out over the next two years would provide them with everything they would need to get an A if they applied it fully in the exams at the end of the course. I explained this to them in the first lesson that I taught them, and then I set them their first homework: to write me a letter, dated on the day of their GCSE results, explaining what they had done over the previous two years that had enabled them to get the A that they had achieved. Quite a few of them struggled to understand the chronology of this – it took some explaining. But, eventually, they grasped the idea and set about their task.

The following week, I collected the homework in. It was, undoubtably, the best homework task I have ever set. The students, without exception, identified the approaches they would need to take to learning and study over the next two years in order to excel. Several of them identified specific aspects of their English work that they knew they would need to fix. More than one identified aspects of their behaviour that they would need to keep in check. And a significant number wrote about their confidence and self-image. Here is one example:

Dear Mr Hildrew

I went to get my GCSE results today. I was over the moon when I found out I had got an A in english. I think I got an A in english because I had a growth mindset. I believed in myself and I challenged myself to do better or aim higher whenever I got any test results back. Instead of being threatened by other people getting higher than me, I was inspired.[7]

This was the first piece of work in every student's exercise book. It helped me immensely in getting to know the students, giving me an "in" to discussing their approaches to learning right from the first lesson. Periodically through the year, I would return them to the letter they had written, to refocus them on the strategies and approaches they had said they would need to adopt if they were going to succeed, holding them to account for when they fell short of the expectations they had of themselves. And I kept my end of the bargain, resolutely only using the top-band criteria in all of my lessons throughout the course, setting my expectation of their work only at A and A* standard. When they fell short of that standard, I provided feedback to support them in closing the gap between what they had produced and the top-band expectation I had of them. But above all we focused on attitude and approach, and the kind of study habits they would need to succeed.

The effectiveness of this approach is that it directly tackles belief in success. From the beginning of the course, I made it clear that an A was my expectation and that I would be teaching to A grade standard throughout, supporting students to close the gap between their current performance and that expectation. What they did in their first homework was to visualise success and identify for themselves the approaches they would need to take to enable that success. Making that eventual destination concrete at the very start of their exercise books created a possible reality where they could get an A, and over time, they worked closer and closer to it.

Why I don't like the word "ability"

Most schools I've worked in talk about "high-ability" students, "middle-ability" students, and "low-ability" students. They talk about teaching "mixed ability" groups or "setting by ability." This is a damaging label. When you talk about a mixed ability group, what are you really saying? That some of them are more "able" than others? This language implies that your "low-ability" students are actually less able to improve. The word itself reinforces the widening of the gap. In actual fact, as we all know, students who end up labelled "low ability" have complex needs, some cognitive, some behavioural, some social, and some attitudinal, which have led to them performing poorly. This poor performance – their prior attainment – gains them the label of "low ability," but it does not necessarily follow that low attainment corresponds to lack of ability.

In fact, when we are talking about "ability" in schools, we are usually talking about "performance" or "attainment." And, if that's what we're talking about, those are the terms that we should use. Those "low-ability" students are actually low attaining. It isn't a life sentence. They can improve. What needs to change in order to improve their attainment? Is there some provision we can put in place? Or is it something that they need to change about their approach or attitude?

Ability is not fixed. As teachers, we can work with young people to overcome their cognitive, behavioural, social, and attitudinal issues and improve their ability to access the curriculum. We certainly won't solve all of those issues outright, but we can ameliorate them – and we must. But labelling a young person as "low ability" is not going to motivate them or us to try.

Notes

1 Gunderson et al., "Parent praise to 1- to 3-year-olds."
2 In particular see: Haimovitz & Dweck ("What predicts children's fixed and growth intelligence mind-sets?") on parents' reactions to failure; Park et al. ("Young children's motivational frameworks and math achievement") on how teacher expectations influence student motivation.
3 This figure, posted by Albert Mehrabian in *Silent Messages,* is not actually true of all situations.
4 Duckworth cites this experience in *Grit*, page 184.
5 Yeager et al., "Breaking the cycle of mistrust."
6 Zander described this strategy in a Teacher's TV strand called "Gurus."
7 I was so moved by this particular piece that I tweeted it: https://twitter.com/chrishil drew/status/512999024925110272

Bibliography

Duckworth, A. (2016). *Grit.* London: Vermilion.

Gunderson, E. A., Dweck, C. S., Gripshover, S. A., Romero, C., Goldin-Meadow, S., & Levine, S.C. (2013). Parent praise to 1- to 3-year-olds predicts children's motivational frameworks 5 years later. *Child Development*, *84*(5), 1–16.

Haimovitz, K., & Dweck, C. S. (2016). What predicts children's fixed and growth intelligence mind-sets? Not the parents' views of intelligence but their parents' views of failure. *Psychological Science*, *27*(6), 859–869.

Mehrabian, A. (1972). *Silent Messages.* Belmont, CA: Wadsworth Publishing.

Park, D., Gunderson, E. A., Tsukayama, E., Levine, S. C., & Beilock, S. L. (2016). Young children's motivational frameworks and math achievement: Relation to teacher-reported instructional practices, but not teacher theory of intelligence. *Journal of Educational Psychology*, *108*(3), 300–313.

Yeager, D. S., Cohen, G. L., Garcia, J., Purdie-Vaughns, V., Apfel, N., Brzustoski, P., et al. (2014). Breaking the cycle of mistrust: Wise interventions to provide critical feedback across the racial divide. *Journal of Experimental Psychology*, *143*(2), 804–824.

Zander, B. (2006, 10 July). Benjamin Zander: Gurus. Retrieved 10 April, 2017, from *TeachFind*: http://archive.teachfind.com/ttv/www.teachers.tv/videos/benjamin-zander.html

Marking, assessment, and feedback with a growth mindset

Let's begin this chapter by agreeing the terms. For the purposes of this book, **marking** is the process of checking, correcting, and giving a mark to a piece of work. The mark can simply be a tick, a check that "this work has been done"; or it could be a numerical mark, a grade, or a judgment of some kind. This process can lead to **assessment**, which is the process of evaluating and measuring the performance of learners in the tasks you have set them. In summative assessment, the process stops here. In formative assessment, however, it is followed by **feedback**. Feedback is when students receive advice or instruction about their performance in order to develop and improve it. The three processes are interlinked and inform one another, but they are distinct and separate and need to be considered as such.

In a growth mindset school, and indeed in learning more generally, the emphasis falls heaviest on feedback. Constructive feedback is the essential ingredient that helps all learners move forward. However, receiving critique can be a challenging experience. In earlier chapters, I wrote about the importance of encouraging purposeful effort in order to improve performance. If the work has been the result of substantial effort, receiving critique on its flaws can be difficult. "I tried really hard, and it's still not right," the inner voice might say. But one of the central principles of the growth mindset can be found in the response to critique and feedback. If a growth mindset is the belief that intelligence and ability is not fixed but can be developed, then every experience becomes a learning experience. You approach every task with the attitude "how can I learn from this?" or "how can this help me to improve?" Beginning the task with this attitude means that the critique is an integral part of the process. The task is not over when you have completed the work; it is only over when you have received the feedback and acted on it in order to improve, and complete the learning that you set out to do. Shifting the mindset away from the "it's finished when I put my pen down" approach is one of the primary jobs in developing a growth mindset culture.

One way to achieve this is to always emphasise the process over the product. When setting up a learning task, explain what the learning points are and what the process of completing the task is designed to teach, develop, or provide the opportunity to practise. Continue to emphasise this throughout the process, but especially at the end. At the familiar cry of "I've finished," challenge the students to explain exactly what it is they have finished: The task? The work? Or the learning? Only when they have received, and acted on, the feedback is the learning process completed. And even then, given the cyclical nature of teaching and learning, it is likely to lead to a further task to take the learning forward to the next stage. As we soon realise, the cathedral is never really finished.

In this sense, many of the "famous failures" demonstrations and examples which are often used to illustrate a growth mindset approach miss the point. Michael Jordan's celebrated 1997 advertisement for Nike is often held up as an example here. In the commercial, the famous basketball star gets out of a car and walks, in moody slow motion, into a stadium, under the voice-over:

> I've missed more than nine thousand shots in my career. I've lost almost three hundred games. Twenty-six times, I've been trusted to take the game-winning shot and missed. I've failed over and over and over again in my life. And that is why I succeed.

What the commercial is emphasising is not the failure in and of itself, but what Michael Jordan learned from the failure. The feedback he received and the lessons he learned from missing those shots allowed him to improve and develop his game. His own self-talk – illustrated perfectly in the voice-over – also provided valuable feedback and helped to develop the resilience within his character that enabled a never-give-up attitude both on and off the court. The same goes for Steve Jobs, famously fired from Apple at age 30; or Walt Disney, fired from his newspaper job for "lacking imagination" and having "no original ideas"; or the Beatles, rejected from Decca with the words "they have no future in show business." Each of these is a great example of resilience and refusal to give up. They are paragons of grit and determination. But equally, these experiences occurred early in their careers and show that in those formative years, the process was all important. Whilst honing your craft, learning and developing, imperfection is inevitable. Setbacks cannot be avoided. Your reaction to them is what matters the most.

In relating this back to the classroom, it is worth considering what emphasis we place on the process and what emphasis we place on the product. I have certainly been guilty of overemphasising the value of the final product in far too many of my lessons. A case in point that always springs to mind is the tea-stained letter. I'm sure I can't be alone in having undertaken this task with my classes. When reading a work of literature set in the past, I have asked the students to write in role as one of the characters for homework. I have mentioned, in passing, that they can present their work as if it were on paper from the original time of the text. The children go home and soak their white A4 in used teabags. Some will do this before they have written on it and let it dry. Others will make the mistake of applying the tea after their writing, unintentionally demonstrating the scientific process of chromatography on their pen ink. The more adventurous might char the edges of their paper with a match; one or two might let this get out of control and then apologise for burning out most of paragraph three when they hand their homework in the next day. And what happens when they hand it in? I am thrilled. I heap praise on them for all the effort they have put in. I'm especially impressed with the couple of really keen students who have rolled their work up into a scroll and tied it with a ribbon, even though they're actually impossible to fit into my marking folder and they'll roll off my pile of books as I try to get them back to the office.

Humour aside, it's worth considering the feedback I am providing here. What I am saying in my reaction is that I value the product they have made. The tea-staining, the edge-charring, the calligraphy in the old-fashioned script they've used for their heading – these are the things that have impressed me. Now, if that was what I was setting out to teach them, there may be some value in it. But I have never taught a lesson with the objective "how to make a piece of plain A4 look like Tudor-era parchment." My lesson objective would far more likely have been "to demonstrate empathy with the protagonist" or "to write in role in order to demonstrate understanding of the distinctive voice of the character." If the learning was what mattered, this is what I should value. This is what I should emphasise. The struggles that the students had with writing in role, the moments where they had successfully captured the character's voice and those where they had lapsed back into informality or modern English; the moments where they had demonstrated clear understanding of the protagonist's moral dilemmas, or those where they had misunderstood their relationships with the other characters – these should be the aspects of the task that I value, and these should therefore be the areas where I provide feedback and critique. The tea-staining is a distraction. But the work which goes up on the exemplar-work wall display in my classroom has, in the past, usually been the one that is presented the best and which contains the fewest errors. The ones which get closest to perfection. The ones where the only feedback is celebration and praise.

In a growth mindset school, this needs to be reversed. If a piece of work contains no errors or approaches perfection, the task that has been set needs to be more challenging. What should be celebrated and put on the exemplar-work wall display is the piece with the whole of the third paragraph covered in crossings-out and corrections, with an asterisk leading to a much-needed revision and addition at the bottom of the final page which raises the standard of the writing considerably. The tea-staining and scroll-rolling is lovely, of course, but what have they learned from it? And could they have devoted their time and energy to the quality of the writing they produced, rather than its presentation?

Austin's Butterfly and a feedback culture

The work of Ron Berger is well worth exploring in order to understand how to build a school culture which values the process of learning first and the product second.

His book *An Ethic of Excellence* is subtitled *Building a Culture of Craftsmanship with Students*. His approach is to insist on excellence as a standard in all aspects of work in schools, including purposeful projects with tangible outcomes guided by repeated critique sessions in peer and expert groups. Berger's critique protocols are no less brilliant for their simplicity:

- Be kind

- Be specific

- Be helpful[1]

Berger's approach to critique feedback is best demonstrated in his oft-cited example of "Austin's Butterfly."[2] This video, shared by Expeditionary Learning, shows Berger working through the process of drawing a butterfly undertaken by a first-grade boy called Austin from Boise, Idaho, in 2002. Berger tells the story of Austin's Butterfly to students of different ages from Presumpscot Elementary School in Portland, Maine. He shows the model that Austin was working from: a photograph of a tiger swallowtail butterfly. He then shows six drafts of the drawing that Austin made, seeking from the students the kind, specific, and helpful critique that allowed Austin to improve his butterfly drawing. From the initial, imprecise, childlike representation, the process draws out a scientifically accurate eye and eventually, by draft six, an impressively accurate drawing of the tiger swallowtail. I am certain that Berger's choice of a butterfly for this oft-repeated example is not accidental, as the narrative reveals excellence emerging from the chrysalis of amateurism with all the awe and wonder that this metamorphosis deserves.

In my description of Austin's drafts, I quite deliberately used the adjective "childlike" to describe his first attempt. Because, of course, at the time of drawing the butterfly Austin would have been between 6 and 7 years old. There would doubtless be many who would have accepted that first, inexact representation as a finished piece, and perhaps even praised Austin for the work he had done. As Berger himself says, "it's not bad, and it *is* a butterfly." But beneath the surface of the video, and explicitly in *An Ethic of Excellence,* Berger critiques this approach. The first butterfly is not good enough. It isn't what the task required. He was asked to produce a "scientific drawing of [the] butterfly," but "he forgot to look like a scientist" and drew, instead, the image of a butterfly he had in his head. When I first saw Berger explaining this, I was struck by the number of times in my career when I had accepted the first butterfly as the finished piece. Grateful, perhaps, that my students had attempted the task, and seeing that they had achieved some understanding or fulfilled some aspects of what I was looking for, I would dutifully mark the work, perhaps offering a few words of advice about how to improve it. "Make sure you read my comments," I would say, thinking "because I spent a long time writing them and I don't want all that work to be wasted." But then I would say, "in today's lesson, we're moving on to . . ."; in that instant, all of that feedback would be wasted no matter how carefully the students read it.

What Berger shows us is that if we want our feedback to have impact, we must give time over for students to act upon that feedback. He also shows us that it is not the teacher who is necessarily the arbiter of all feedback but that carefully managed and focused peer feedback can have an equally, if not more, dynamic effect on improving student work. And, of course, he shows us that it is simply not good enough to accept the first butterfly. In doing so, we lower expectations of what students can achieve, and we leave the potential for excellence untapped, undiscovered, and unknown. Because if we think that that crude sketch is all we should be expecting of 6- or 7-year-olds, we are doing them a disservice; they are capable of much, much more.

Accepting the first butterfly also has a corrosive effect on the culture of learning in a school. It normalises the idea that we are supposed to get it right first time and that our first attempt is what will be assessed, logged, filed, and accepted. As the acronym shows us, the First Attempt In Learning is far more likely to be a "FAIL," and in Berger's approach, it is this which is normalised. For the students at Presumpscot and the other Expeditionary Learning Schools in America, the notion that your first attempt at something is only a starting point is part of their learning approach. They *expect* to redraft their work. As a second-grader called Hadley says in the Austin's Butterfly video, "He made six drafts . . . we can make other drafts if it's not right." This culture of continuous improvement embeds the key features of the growth mindset – that we embrace challenges, persist in the face of setbacks, see effort as the path to mastery, and learn from criticism – within the very culture of the classroom and normalises them.

In order to achieve this culture, we need to rethink the way we approach feedback. The advent of "DIRT" – Dedicated Improvement and Reflection Time – over recent years goes some way to embedding this. In DIRT, feedback on a piece of work is phrased as a series of questions or additional improvement or revision tasks, which students are then given the opportunity to complete within the classroom or at home. This space and time ensures that the messages from the feedback result in direct student activity, designed to help embed the improvements and refinements needed on the initial piece. It also allows the teacher to check whether those improvements and refinements have been completed and whether misunderstandings or misconceptions have been adequately addressed. Done well, DIRT is a powerful thing to witness, and it can lead to fruitful and inspiring ongoing dialogue in the student book. The work becomes a living text, almost like a blog or online video where the debate continues in the comments section below the line. However, there is also a risk that DIRT, when it is entirely teacher-driven, can become a workload vacuum because the teacher is not only required to provide feedback on the new work completed in the exercise book, but also to provide feedback on the DIRT tasks completed in response to the previous piece of feedback. It is easy to see how this may soon spiral out of control.

In Berger's approach, however, the students themselves have been trained to provide kind, specific, and helpful feedback in small "critique groups." Making reference to the established success criteria and using successful exemplar models as templates, the students suggest iterative improvements on draft after draft, learning not only how to improve their own work but also how to apply the success criteria more specifically and, therefore, empowering them to self-correct, develop, and improve their own work. There is teacher assessment too – often in the form of presentations – but much of the feedback is provided verbally and captured not in purple or green pen in an exercise book, but in the iterative improvement of the work itself. The notion that the lengthy written dialogue of teacher comment, student response, teacher comment on the student response, and student response to the teacher comment on the student response is in some way necessary to "show progress" is one which speaks of a culture more interested in accountability than learning. The perceptive professional looking at a record of student work will see the improvement in the work and recognise that the feedback is having an impact, even if the feedback is not written. There are no written comments on the six versions of Austin's Butterfly, but the progress is there for all to see.

However, even with DIRT successfully embedded in classroom practice and the potential workload issues under control, the very nature of curriculum planning means that improvement and reflection is still likely to be marginal. DIRT addresses that moment in my earlier example when I implored my class to please read my comments so my hours of marking were not wasted, but it does not address the next step: "in today's lesson, we're moving on to . . . ." For instance, if we had been working on writing to argue and persuade and I had marked a draft of a persuasive speech and provided feedback and DIRT time but then moved on later in the lesson to a different topic, the chance to properly develop the skills and knowledge embedded in the feedback loop would be curtailed. In order to give the students the best chance of really mastering the topic being taught, the drive to "move on" needs to be held back to allow this to happen. The medium-term planning for the unit needs to prioritise those elements of skills or knowledge which will be subject to those iterative, looped redrafting and development processes, and students need to be given the space and time within that curriculum plan to allow for mastery to develop. Inevitably, there will always be a "moving on" moment, but if the curriculum requires you to move on before the students have achieved the level of mastery you know they will need, any future learning will be built on an unstable foundation, and sooner or later somebody is going to have to go back to fix it. Taking the time in the early stages might seem problematic when there is so much to do and so much to cover – but not taking the time runs the risk of undermining the foundations of the cathedral.

The link between assessment and feedback

Any kind of helpful feedback requires an accurate assessment. In order to say what has been successful and which aspects require development or improvement, a judgment has to be made about the qualities of the work. In order for this assessment to be made accurately and for the feedback to be helpful and specific, the person making the assessment needs to have a clear and precise idea of what a good piece of work looks like or what the success criteria for such work would be. In some cases this will be a clear-cut right or wrong: "you've got this calculation wrong, so the figures which follow are incorrect." In others, judgments will be more subjective: "I'm not sure that you've got the balance of light and shade right here; I think the left-hand side of the picture is too dark and it unbalances the composition." However, in all cases, that assessment judgment precedes the kind, helpful, and specific feedback which allows the learner to improve, develop, and progress.

This is the process which is widely known as "formative assessment." This is a term most widely associated with Dylan Wiliam and Paul Black since their seminal 1998 booklet *Inside the Black Box* explored the notion that this single feature was "at the heart of effective teaching."[3] The principle of formative assessment is that the assessment provides

> information to be used as feedback to modify the teaching and learning activities in which [teachers and students] are engaged. *Such assessment becomes "formative assessment" when the evidence is actually used to adapt the teaching work to meet the needs.*[4]

It goes without saying, I hope, that the assessment therefore has to be accurate in order for the feedback to be used to modify teaching and learning activities effectively.

This has several implications for effective feedback, but more fundamentally for effective assessment. First, a simple "good work" clearly won't cut it. Whilst that may be kind, it is neither specific nor helpful. Precision in identifying what it is about a particular piece of work which is successful or which is not yet successful enables effective feedback. But how precise can we be?

The first port of call for many teachers when asked to assess how successful, or otherwise, a piece of work has been, will be a specification or examination mark scheme. These rubrics provide the success criteria against which students' final summative assessments will be judged and, therefore, provide the framework through which we wish students to progress in order to demonstrate their attainment. This is a sensible and entirely appropriate approach, and student familiarity with the assessment rubrics against which they are judged can only be helpful in order for them to successfully jump the academic hoops in their final exam hall. It is also the case that exam boards devise these rubrics carefully and rigorously with the weight of significant subject expertise and academic research behind them, quality assured by the regulators and refined over decades of experience. However, an examination mark scheme or specification assessment rubric is not the only measure with which assessments can be made.

Until 2013, the National Curriculum in England was accompanied by an assessment rubric all of its own. National Curriculum levels were actually called "attainment targets" within the curricula launched in 1999 and 2007. In the 1999 National Curriculum, it was clearly explained that "an attainment target sets out the knowledge, skills and understanding that pupils of different abilities and maturities are expected to have by the end of each key stage"[5] as provided for in the Education Act 1996, section 353a. I would certainly question whether this ambition in itself was compatible with a growth mindset approach, as it enshrined within it the notion that pupils have "different abilities" in the first place and led to assumptions that a child achieving at a certain level at one point within the curriculum is thenceforth limited to the equivalent level in other and future aspects of it. However, even this intention was soon subverted, and what replaced it was potentially even more damaging. Those end-of-key-stage expectations soon became the standard against which all work was judged, divided up into sublevels and applied out of context to individual pieces of student writing, mathematics, speech, music, history, and geography work, and soon to children themselves. Not only was a piece of work given a level 3a or 4c, but the whole child was labelled with that level. "They're a 4c in English but a 5b in Maths. What are we going to do about it?"

This was clearly not what National Curriculum attainment targets were designed to do, and their gradual deconstruction and division into tiny, assessment-focus-linked tick boxes soon overbalanced the teaching and learning agenda. Teachers, and whole-school systems, became increasingly reliant on the National Curriculum's assessment framework as the means to deliver formative assessment, but ended up chasing shadows as the behemoth of A3-sized APP (assessing pupils' progress) grids became the norm. Part of the issue was thinking that it was possible to distil a subject with the breadth of English or Mathematics down to a series of tightly focused criteria-referenced statements. In fact, such an attempt is fruitless. Even the exam specifications only assess tightly focused aspects of the subjects through carefully targeted questions and tasks. In planning and teaching, I have found the latter approach to be the most helpful. Think about what it is that the students are going to be learning today. Teach them that. Provide them with clear success criteria for the tasks they will be undertaking, and assess them against those criteria. Provide them with feedback to help them to improve their work. It seems so simple – but it's so easy to get lost in the morass of spreadsheets, trackers, and monitoring points. The simplicity can rapidly become very complex.

None of the above requires putting a grade or level against a piece of work. Wiliam and Black's research would indicate that doing so is, in fact, counterproductive.[6] One of their key findings, and one which has significant implications for students' mindsets, is the difference between feedback which is ego-involving and that which is task-involving. Giving out grades or levels invites comparison with others and leads to the establishment of a rank-order or hierarchy within the classroom. When it relates simply to one piece of work, it is possible to couch such grading in careful conditions and to explain that one piece of work does not define you. Such an approach does not, of course, prevent this from happening. Certainly, I have had the experience of students being disheartened by the receipt of a grade, even upset. Alternatively, I have seen students in my own classes celebrating with a fist pump when an assessment has come back with a level 5.6, proudly declaring, "Yes! I was a 5.3 last time!" Without going into the detail of the nonsense of awarding a single piece of work a subdivided level based on an arbitrary end-of-key-stage expectation for National Curriculum attainment by students of different abilities and maturities, the reaction itself is demonstrably ego-involving. The celebration – or the tears – shows the young person's emotional involvement with the act of assessment. And what Wiliam and Black suggest is that once the emotions have been triggered in this way, the chances of engaging that young person in the commentary which accompanies the grade – that formative feedback designed to help the learner improve – are slim to none. The research they have conducted shows this kind of feedback has no positive effect on the students at all and can even have a negative effect. What this means is that students would do just as well or better with no feedback at all than if provided with this kind of ego-involving feedback which invites comparison with others.

The implications of this are profound. I have spent years of my career levelling students' work, wrestling over best-fit criteria when they were hitting level 5c in one assessment focus but only level 4b in another, rebuilding damaged confidence from a poor grade, and trying to break through the defensive wall built by those students who only ever received the lowest grades – and it turns out the students could actually have done better if I hadn't bothered at all. So why does this happen? The theory suggests that when receiving feedback, students make a choice. They either choose to engage in activities which will help them to learn and grow or they choose to protect their well-being. If their first reaction is emotional, in order to protect themselves and restore their sense of well-being, students will devote their mental energy to the activities which will provide that for them. This might be poor behaviour, perhaps screwing the work up or defacing it in some way. It might be laughter, mocking themselves and their poor performance in order to make light of it and diminish the impact. It could be tears, or silence, or pretending that the problem simply doesn't exist. None of these reactions helps with learning. All of them entrench a fixed mindset by devoting energy to avoidance strategies rather than learning.

The alternative to ego-involving feedback is to provide feedback which causes thinking and promotes learning. This is task-involving feedback. This kind of feedback identifies what was done well, what needed improving, and, vitally, how to go about making those improvements. Where this kind of feedback is normalised, the classroom culture promotes the growth mindset. The feedback is implying that all classroom work is an attempt at learning and that there is always progress and improvement which can be made. When receiving feedback in such a culture, students are far more likely to respond to the receipt of any work by looking for the opportunities to learn than for signifiers of their status or position within the group. The only competition that they have in such a culture is with themselves, competing for continuous improvement. They see value in the work as part of an ongoing learning process, rather than seeing the product as something which defines them as a person.

Taking this approach to its logical conclusion means un-thinking many aspects of school culture. The receipt of grades on pieces of work is so normalised within schools that unpicking it is a feat of re-education for teachers, students, and families. But it is necessary work. The grade serves no learning function at all. It serves to mark position – but it does not help learning. Teacher assessment of student strengths and areas for development and improvement should of course continue, and I recognise that there may well need to be a system for recording this as it is not possible to hold all of the information in the memory, but it does not require a complex system of levelling, grading, or subdivisions. In its simplest terms it means that the teacher and the student need to understand what they know and what they can do, what they don't know and can't do yet, and what they are going to do next to close that gap. None of this requires them to know anything about their current grade. In fact, adding this information into the mix is not only surplus to requirements but, as it is ego-involving, may in fact be counterproductive.

Interestingly, recent developments in the external examination system in England have actually helped in this area. Since 2010, the qualification, exams and assessment regulator Ofqual has been revising the assessment framework. This manifested initially in the removal of National Curriculum levels, replaced instead in each section of the curriculum with the simple phrase: "by the end [of the key stage] pupils are expected to know, apply and understand the matters, skills and processes specified in the relevant programme of study." Whilst many schools have rushed to reinvent levels, labelling students or pieces of work as "emerging," "developing," or "secure" instead of "level 3," "level 4," or "level 5," such approaches miss the point. We no longer have to put labels, levels, or grades on work or students. All we need to do is provide feedback to help them to improve.

The second strand to Ofqual's reforms involved the revision of the GCSE specifications, moving to a statistically generated grading system using the numbers 9–1 as a replacement for the existing A*–G system. When I started teaching GCSE English, there were clear criteria linked to each grade. You needed to show certain skills and qualities, and if you did, you would get that grade. For example, in the OCR English Literature syllabus from the year 2000,[7] if you wrote a "detailed, sometimes analytical response, beginning to express critical views," you would be awarded a grade B. If you were to "make convincing critical responses with some evidence of original thought," you would get a grade A. And if, as we would hope, you began "to advance personal theories and to respond critically and at length to narrowly focused sections of texts," you would be putting yourself in line for an A*. With such detail and certainty, it would be possible to award grades to individual student responses. But the new system for GCSEs relies instead on the system of comparable outcomes.

Mark schemes such as that cited above still exist, but they are only used to award numerical marks to responses. The grade boundaries are only assigned nationally after all of the exams are assessed and the marks are awarded, based on a slew of statistical information including the prior attainment of that cohort nationally and their performance in the examinations across all the different exam boards. Importantly, those grade boundaries are cohort specific: what gets a grade 6 one year will not necessarily get a grade 6 the next. This means that it is now not only impossible but also substantially misleading to grade students' work at GCSE. Teachers cannot possibly know what grade a response will receive. Yes, it is possible to say with some accuracy how many marks out of twenty a response would receive according to the examination mark scheme, but any suggestion of a grade would be educated guesswork at best. This has naturally caused some alarm for teachers, who were used to being able to predict grades with some degree of reliability. It has certainly caused consternation for senior leaders, whose complex in-year tracking spreadsheets with colour-coded flags to identify those at risk of underachievement relied entirely on those reliable predictions. But for teachers with an eye on mindset theory, the impossibility of accurately grading students' work should be seen as liberation. Since we now can't grade, we must instead focus on what students are doing well and what they need to improve. We need to keep teaching them, keep helping them to improve, until they reach the end of Year 11 and walk into the examination hall at the peak of their performance, knowing exactly what they need to do to tackle the exam to the very best of their current ability. And it is only then, in that examination hall, that the product finally matters more than the process. That examination is no longer an opportunity for receiving feedback, learning, and growing. For the first and last time – until A-level at least – it is a summative assessment where the student's final performance is judged, fed into a national statistical database, and ranked in a hierarchy with every other 16-year-old born within the same September to August window as they were. We, and they, hope that they have learned enough to get the outcome that they deserve. But whilst this might be the final destination within our school system, up until that point, the process is all, and every assessment should be an opportunity for learning and growth through task-involving feedback which prioritises the growth mindset.

Targets

When I launched growth mindset with staff for the first time, one of the first reactions I got was from our Head of Geography, who rushed over to say: "does this mean we're getting rid of Challenge Grades?" Challenge Grades was our term for targets, which we had been using to drive aspiration in the school over the previous five years. Her point was, essentially, that sharing target grades with students was incompatible with a growth mindset. Why is this?

To understand why this might be, it's worth considering how the targets themselves are generated. At secondary level, at least in every secondary school I've worked in, the base data for all student targets tends to be FFT: the Fischer Family Trust. The Fischer Family Trust works with the national pupil database of test and exam results across whole cohorts of students and tracks their performance. They have been doing this since 2004, building up a bank of expertise and statistical information to allow them to model how likely it is that a student with particular characteristics (gender, date of birth, and so on) and particular results at the end of primary school will get particular grades at secondary school. This is an incredibly useful service, providing really valuable statistical analysis based on a truly comprehensive data set. Recently, they introduced a new version of their software, FFT Aspire, which allows schools to use the database to set student-level targets within the school's cohort. It's really mind-blowing stuff.

Except, of course, for the fact that it doesn't really work. I don't blame Fischer Family Trust for this, because actually they couldn't be clearer in the material they publish. Within their original software, called FFT Live, they were at pains to point out how their data should be used. In a help sheet called "Using reports appropriately and effectively," they say: "the estimates . . . can be used to **support** the process of target setting, but **should not** take the place of target setting." Not content with just emboldening the type, the guide sheet concludes with some strident capitals: "**remember, use the reports ALONGSIDE other data, your own professional judgement and aspirations AND THE ASPIRATIONS AND MOTIVATIONS OF CHILDREN THEMSELVES.**"[8] In other words, the data alone is nothing. For the target setting process to be successful, human intervention is required. It takes professional judgment to set a student target. FFT have continued to emphasise this as they upgraded their service to Aspire. On their web page, they show a clear graphic which says:

Estimate + Professional Knowledge = Prediction; Prediction + Challenge = Target.[9]

But so many schools and school leaders miss out the first part of the equation. Without the time to sit and exercise their professional judgment in the case of every student in the cohort in relation to every subject they are taking, it is so much easier to just import the targets wholesale into the school's management software, add some challenge, and consider target setting done.

The problem with this approach is that whilst the massive data set from the national pupil database enables FFT to make legitimate estimates, that data set is comprised of thousands of thousands of individuals. The general estimates, in essence, provide the most likely outcome for similar students nationally. There are filters you can use to tweak those estimates to the top 20 per cent of similar students or the top 5 per cent of similar students, but still the mathematics behind the estimate is taking an average of thousands of other students. When turned into a target grade, that estimate applies back to one individual. And there is absolutely no guarantee that the individual in question will be in any way "average."

We used this approach to our advantage when we worked with the Biscuit Club. There we showed each boy their FFT Live estimates page. An example is shown in Table 10.1.

Table 10.1 Example "chance chart" from FFT Live (not from one of the Biscuit Club!)

Name	DoB	Est Basis	Subject Group	\% chance of achieving KS4 Grade								\% chance		Grades		
				G+	F+	E+	D+	C+	B+	A+	A*	A*-C	Pass	GM	HGM	GA
		SE	Science	99.%	99.%	99.%	99.%	97.5%	81.5%	47.4%	13.7%	97.5%	99.%	B	47.4%	A
		SE	Science	99.%	99.%	99.%	99.%	98.8%	88.7%	59.6%	21.5%	98.8%	99.%	A	21.5%	S

We used tables like this to work with individuals to help them to think about what they would need to change about their own behaviour, strategies, and approach to make themselves one of the minority of similar students who went on to get the highest grades, rather than one of the majority. At this level, when discussing the estimates and thinking about possibilities with individuals, the data can be very powerful. But, if the student only sees a B grade and that is the target that they are set, the notion of possibility evaporates. If the chances of exceeding that B grade are never spoken of, they cease to exist for that student, capping their aspiration at a particular point when they could, of course, be capable of more.

The reverse is also true, because there will be students within each cohort for whom FFT *over*estimates what they are capable of achieving. If the target is set too high, it becomes a constant reminder of inadequacy, and no matter how hard the student tries and how much effort they apply, they experience disappointment and failure at every step, crying out "you can't" with every assessment, report, and exam, no matter how much progress has been made. In this scenario, the repeated experience of failure can lead the student to believe that, actually, effort does not lead to success and that, in fact, they just don't have the ability to achieve. In this way, the overambitious target generates fixed mindset thinking, dampens aspiration, and switches students off to learning.

The use of large statistical data sets forgets the individual. That is their nature. But, in the growth mindset school, the focus is all on the individual and their beliefs about their own learning capacity. The notion that you can use statistics to extrapolate the potential of an individual is profoundly flawed. It will give you a frame of reference, perhaps, but it cannot give you a grade with any reliability. To do so poses a risk to the students' mindset. Set the target too high and the student enters a fixed mindset due to repeated failure to achieve. Set it too low and the student easily reaches the target without having to try, failing to reinforce the connection between effort and achievement. Like Goldilocks and the three bears, it is likely that the algorithm will set some of the targets "just right," but that is more by luck than judgment. In a growth mindset school, therefore, publishing target grades to students risks damage more than it promotes growth.

So what should we do instead? First, we should challenge the fallacy that we can ever really know what a student's potential might be. We could share the "chance charts" with every student, but in my experience this is an unmanageable task and, at scale, proves problematic. Instead, rather than aiming for some spurious and potentially arbitrary grade in some distant future, it is preferable to deal with known quantities. One known quantity is a student's current attainment: we should be able to accurately assess what students know and don't know, what they can do and can't do, what they can apply and what they can't apply. We can then provide them with feedback on how to improve. When we next assess them, we should be able to identify the progress they have made and give them feedback on the next steps. Then we should repeat that process. And repeat it again. And keep going, with the students getting better and better until . . . well, until we run out of time. Not until they hit their target grade – but until there is simply no school left for them to improve within.

There is a place for those data-driven targets and flight paths behind the scenes. As we look at the progress the students are making, we can use those large data sets to make a judgment about whether they are progressing far enough fast enough, compared to their similar peers nationally. We can make inferences about students who are not progressing far enough fast enough, and we may be able to plan approaches, strategies, and interventions which would help them get back on track, but we must remember that progress is unlikely to be linear and smooth for the individual and that a setback is not the same as a catastrophe. Using this data behind the scenes can inform teaching, helping to benchmark progress against a cohort average. But comparing the individual's progress to the average progress of a similar cohort is a different proposition from applying that average progress (plus some degree of "appropriate challenge") back to an individual as a motivational tool.

As with any change related to becoming a growth mindset school, taking the targets away requires a cultural shift. It requires a cultural shift for teachers, who for years, have been used to being held accountable for the proportion of their students achieving their FFT grades and who, at the request of their leaders, get the students to write their target grades inside their new exercise books in the first lesson of every school year. It requires a cultural shift for the students, who have unquestioningly written the grades in their exercise books and filled in their assessment grades underneath, looking perhaps with horror, amusement, or indifference at the similarity between the grade they are getting now and the grade which Sir or Miss had told them they are capable of. And it requires a cultural shift for families, accustomed as they have been to either celebrating, commiserating, rebuking, or perhaps ignoring the reports which come home showing which subjects their child is on target, below target, or above target in. Culture shift takes time, but it is achievable. Presenting a clear rationale for the change – which I hope I have done – is essential. Replace the target-driven reports with a helpful progress check that takes two known data points – where they were last time and where they are now – alongside an analysis of the student's attitude to learning and some improvement advice. Outstanding progress does not require a target grade. It requires excellent teaching and excellent learning – and that is all.

Notes

1 Berger, *An Ethic of Excellence*, page 93.
2 *Austin's Butterfly* (Dir. D. Grant).
3 Wiliam & Black, *Inside the Black Box*, page 2.
4 Ibid.
5 Department for Education and Employment, *The National Curriculum for England*.
6 For example, in Wiliam, "Enculturating learners into communities of practice."
7 OCR, *GCSE English Literature Syllabus 1501*.
8 This exhortation is from a FFT Live guidance sheet entitled "Using estimate reports with students."
9 FFT, "Setting targets, measuring progress."

Bibliography

Berger, R. (2003). *An Ethic of Excellence*. Portsmouth, NH: Heinemann.

Black, P., Harrison, C., Marshall, B., Wiliam, D., & Lee, C. (2002). *Working Inside the Black Box: Assessment for Learning in the Classroom*. London: GL Assessment.

Department for Education and Employment. (1999). *The National Curriculum for England*. London: Qualifications and Curriculum Authority.

FFT. (2017). Setting targets, measuring progress. Retrieved 8 Febuary, 2017, from *FFT*: www.fft.org.uk/fft-aspire/target-setting.aspx

Grant, D. (Producer). (2012). *Austin's Butterfly: Building Excellence in Student Work* [Motion Picture]. https://vimeo.com/38247060

OCR. (2000). *GCSE English Literature Syllabus 1501*. Cambridge: Cambridge Assessment.

Wiliam, D. (1998, September). Enculturating learners into communities of practice: Raising achievement through classroom assessment. Retrieved 24 December, 2016, from Dylan Wiliam's website: www.dylanwiliam.org/Dylan_Wiliams_website/Papers.html

Wiliam, D., & Black, P. (1998). *Inside the Black Box: Raising Standards Through Classroom Assessment*. London: King's College School of Education.

Wiliam, D., & Black, P. (2009, February). Developing the theory of formative assessment. *Educational Assessment, Evaluation and Accountability, 21*:5, https://doi.org/10.1007/s11092-008-9068-5.

Staff development in a growth mindset school

Staff development is central to the development of a growth mindset culture. If we are expecting our students to develop a growth mindset around their own learning, we need to ensure that we take the same approach to our own practice. This means unlearning what staff development looks like, stripping it back to the basics, and approaching anew the process of continuous professional development.

Fundamental to this process is a reappraisal of what it is that makes a good teacher. In my experience, there is a pervading belief in education that you either are or aren't a "good teacher" – that good teachers are born, not made. I think that this belief comes from the fact that teaching is a profession in which it is easy to invest so much of yourself. By its nature it is a personality-driven profession. Who you are – your quirks, foibles, and idiosyncrasies – is the raw material you use to engage your class, to mould and sculpt the material you are teaching, and to build relationships with your students and your colleagues. Your personality is not something that you can, or should, change, so therefore it follows that you are either born with the teaching gene or you are not.

This is fixed mindset thinking. It presupposes that there is only one personality type that will make a successful teacher, and I know that this is not the case. There are as many types of "good teacher" as there are types of people in the world. I know of teachers whose classrooms are bedecked with bunting, full of flora and fauna, a safe haven of almost maternal love, while next door there is a spartan room ruled with black-and-white simplicity and absolute authoritarian order. Students are devoted in equal measure to both approaches, recognising implicitly the difference but respectful of the shared aim – the success of the students themselves. And where that success is forthcoming, the method of achieving it is really of secondary importance.

Love conquers all

There is, in my experience, one quality that all good teachers share: a love of children and working with them to help them learn. This is the core of all successful educational practice, and it is the primary quality that I am looking for whenever I am recruiting for new teachers or walking through the corridors and classrooms of the school. You can see it in the smiles and laughter of the teachers and their students, but you can also see it in the frowns, rebukes, and reprimands. Children feel it. It is this love which builds the relationships between the student and the teacher, which makes the teacher's disappointment when the child falls short of expectations all the more powerful, and which motivates the child to want to meet those expectations next time. It is this love which makes the sometimes overwhelming challenges of working in a school tolerable and which makes every day in the classroom with children a privilege. It is this love which makes a teacher.

There have been initiatives in the past which have sought to attract the best and brightest graduates, prioritising subject knowledge and academic performance as defining factors in deciding the quality of future teachers. Such an approach follows the international examples of Finland and South Korea, where only high-performing graduates meet the requirements to train as teachers. I do always look carefully at the qualifications listed on job application forms for teaching in the schools I lead, and there is no doubt that a top degree in the teaching subject will be a significant factor in shortlisting candidates for interview – but, for me, it is not the deciding factor. That warmth and enthusiasm for the art, craft, and science of teaching, for helping children to improve themselves, and for dedicating your work to the development of others will overrule the quality of the candidate's subject knowledge every time. Some of the finest teachers I have worked with had third class degrees, but their results were astonishing and their practice the envy of others. And I have seen many candidates for jobs who were impeccable on paper but failed to deliver that all-important energy and spark in person. You might want to become a teacher because you love maths, or it might be because you love working with children. If you have the former, but you don't have the latter, then it will be a challenging career choice. To be successful in teaching, you need both.

The power of practice

Whilst the love of teaching children is at the heart of successful classroom practice, it is not the end of the story. Becoming a consistently good teacher is a long, laborious process. Most people can become competent teachers over the first couple of years in the classroom. Over that time, you develop the routines and strategies required to ensure that classes are orderly, that expectations are clear, and that you can deliver the material that you need to teach. Achieving this, when you first enter the classroom, can simply be a matter of survival. What the research shows, sadly, is that once you can deliver and survive, most teachers stop improving and continue at that level. This "plateau" effect[1] continues despite the best efforts of in-service training days, external providers, new initiatives, and attempts to revolutionise teaching at national, regional, local, and even school level. Why does this happen?

I think the reason is that much of what is called "professional development" in schools is, in fact, anything but. I have lost count of the external courses and Inset days I have been on when an inspirational expert has delivered a powerful presentation to a room full of teachers. I have often enjoyed them, although more often I have been preoccupied with the more useful tasks I could be getting done instead. If truth be told, I have even sometimes got on with those more useful tasks during the presentations themselves. But even when those presentations have been at their most engaging and powerful, I can count on the fingers of one hand those which have significantly changed my practice in the classroom for any significant period of time.

It must be baffling for children in a school in the weeks following an Inset day. Suddenly, without warning, they must get a barrage of teachers all trying out the same brilliant new idea they heard about when the children were off. They must go from lesson to lesson where they are suddenly being asked to draw out complex thinking maps, or to work in collaborative jigsaw groups with specific role cards, or to work out whether their understanding is uni-structural, multi-structural, relational, or extended abstract. They bear it with tolerance, knowing that in a couple of weeks the shiny A4 ring-binder on Miss's or Sir's desk will be moved into a drawer or onto a shelf and they'll get back to normal again. Such is the model of continuous professional development that has persisted throughout my career so far. Little wonder, then, that surveys of CPD in England show that so little of the training provided has significant impact on practice.[2]

These top-down models of professional development, where the expert delivers the material to the group, miss out on the vital element of learning which is required to change practice – and that is practice itself. When we teach students a new skill, we do not expect them to grasp it immediately. In our lesson planning, we provide them with plentiful opportunities to apply that skill in a variety of contexts. If we have planned carefully, the scheme of learning will ensure that the new skills and knowledge are interleaved over future lessons so that students return to them repeatedly, spacing out the practice to ensure that there is maximum retention of what they have learned. But the Inset day model does not provide this for teachers, relying on a single point of input and then returning teachers to the same classrooms with the same students, the same lesson plans and schemes, and no opportunity to return to the new learning. Little wonder, then, that the new ideas are lost.

In order to take a growth mindset approach to staff development, the paradigm needs to be inverted. As Matthew Hood has said,[3] teaching is a performance profession and needs to be approached in the same way as other performance professions such as sport, music, and acting. The skills and techniques required to be truly successful need to be honed through careful rehearsal and deliberate practice, guided by expert coaching. This model for performance improvement has long been established in other fields. We would not expect an athlete to better their personal best without careful training, or a concert pianist to tackle Rachmaninov at sight, or an actor to go on stage without rehearsal, relying only on their natural skill and experience. The oft-cited marginal gains approach of the British cycling team has seen the impact of aggregating small improvements in aspects of performance through detailed analysis, remodelling, and coaching.

The deliberate practice approach was established most authoritatively by K. Anders Ericsson and colleagues in their study of the impact of deliberate practice on expert performance.[4] One part of their study focused on violinists at the Music Academy in West Berlin. In their research, they worked with three groups of violinists. The "best" students were those who, according to their teachers, had the potential for a career as an international soloist. They compared these students with a group of "good" violinists, matched to the "best" students in age and gender. Finally, they studied an equivalent group of students who were specialising in Music Education at the Academy, but who also played the violin. The Music Education department had lower admission standards than the pure violinists' course, and its students were most likely to graduate into music teaching rather than music performance careers. By way of comparison, Ericsson also studied a group of middle-aged violinists who had progressed in their careers with places in Germany's leading symphony orchestras.

What the study found was that the largest factor distinguishing between the performance levels of the three groups of students – the best, the good, and the teachers – was the amount of practice they had done. The teachers averaged around four thousand hours of violin practice over their lifetimes, the good violinists practiced around eight thousand hours, whilst the very best had accrued ten thousand hours of practice by the time they joined the Academy in Berlin. In Ericsson's words, "the differences between expert performers and normal adults reflect a life-long period of deliberate effort to improve performance in a specific domain."[5] Malcolm Gladwell, citing Ericsson's study, called this the "10,000-hour rule," suggesting that it takes this many hours of careful and deliberate practice to become an expert at anything, not just the violin.[6] This theme is taken up by Matthew Syed in his book *Bounce*, applying it to his own elite performance in table tennis and, by extension, across disciplines including chess, baseball, and athletics.[7] Angela Duckworth, too, has found similar evidence for the power of practice in honing and developing performance in fields as diverse as ballet, American football, golf, Scrabble, competitive spelling, radiology, and Morse Code operation.[8] If you want to get really good at anything, it seems, practice really is what makes perfect.

There is an important difference, however, between the practice of teaching and deliberate practice to improve teaching. You do not improve your teaching significantly simply by teaching more. Rivkin, Hanushek, and Kain's exploration of the plateau effect shows that after a couple of years in the classroom, improvements in performance tail off. In order to continue improving, teachers need to carefully and deliberately practice improvements in particular aspects of their teaching, whether this be questioning, explanation, pace, feedback, or any one of the many skills, techniques, and component parts that make up the teacher's role. Careful attention needs to be paid to the specific, focused aspect that the teacher is working on, and time must be given for that practice to embed.

What the research into deliberate practice has shown is that it is an effortful activity that can only be sustained for a limited time each day. It is usually neither motivating nor enjoyable, but it is instrumental in achieving further improvement in performance. What keeps those expert performers practising when others would give up – what gives them Duckworth's X-factor of grit – is the passion for the field they are pursuing and the value that they place on the goal. This is why the love of children and teaching is such an important ingredient in good teaching. It is this which will keep motivating the teacher to continue to improve, knowing that they will get better and it will help the children in their class to get even better too.

What this means is that the traditional model of CPD reserved for Inset days and external courses needs to be completely inverted. The most powerful professional development comes, instead, from the teacher carefully and deliberately practising specific aspects of their teaching on a daily basis, developing and honing their skill through reflection and critique. In a growth mindset school, each lesson is an opportunity to learn – not just for the students, but for the professionals who are delivering it – so that the next time that teacher goes into the classroom they will deliver that lesson a little bit better. And the research shows that this is unlikely to be a quick process, with the best estimates suggesting that elite performance is the result of at least a decade of effort to improve performance through deliberate practice. But the rewards are potentially great, since the effect of an expert teacher is significant, lasting for the children in their class years beyond the time that they had that teacher – sometimes even a lifetime. This is why for those with a passion for working with young people to help them learn in the classroom, we need to provide personalised professional development not just five days per year, but every day that they are teaching.

The importance of coaching

In an example that I like to think of as meta-grit, Angela Duckworth recounts the gritty routine of deliberate practice she undertook in preparation for her TED talk on the subject of grit. She describes the first run-through of the talk with producer Juliet Blake and the leader of TED, Chris Anderson. Expecting effusive praise and encouragement, instead she got critique: "too many syllables. Too many slides. And not enough clear, understandable examples . . . zero suspense." She goes on to recount how she honed the structure and delivery of the talk over many weeks through careful rehearsal and often-painful critique from her family, before eventually delivering a six-minute talk that was very different from the one she had originally planned – and all the better for it. "Watch that talk and you'll see me in flow," she says, continuing:

> Search YouTube for the many rehearsals that preceded it – or, for that matter, footage of *anyone* doing effortful, mistake-ridden, repetitive deliberate

practice – and my guess is you'll come up empty. Nobody wants to show you the hours and hours of becoming. They'd rather show you the highlight of what they've become.[9]

What struck me most on reading Duckworth's account of her preparation for this performance was the fact that on her own, she would have delivered to the audience the original TED talk that she had planned – the one with zero suspense, too many slides, and too many syllables. What allowed her to improve and refine the talk was feedback and critique from experts who know what works in a TED talk and want to make sure that each one is the best it can possibly be. Duckworth, for all that she was a MacArthur Fellow and advisor to the White House, the World Bank, NBA and NFL teams, and Fortune 500 CEOs, was not an expert in TED talks; but she was wise enough to listen to those that were, to act on the feedback that she received, and to work hard to put their advice into practice. In short, she was prepared to be coached.

In teaching, we need to have the same approach. We need coaching from experts if we are going to enable continuous improvement, and as professionals we need to be as open as Angela Duckworth was to the critique and feedback that is offered, taking it as an opportunity to grow. Fortunately, schools are full of teachers who, with the proper training, can act as peer coaches to one another. The coach is there to work with the teacher to identify the areas of practice that the teacher wants to develop and improve, and then to work with that teacher to help them stay focused on the improvement goal. The teacher can themselves work as a coach, either in a reciprocal arrangement with the same colleague, in a triad, or across a network of teachers.

A coach is important because, even with the best will in the world, it is difficult to identify areas of your own practice which could be tweaked and improved when you are in the middle of teaching a lesson. There may well be obvious things that you notice: perhaps you misjudged that piece of verbal feedback; maybe you should have given more thinking time before taking the class response to your questioning; perhaps cold-calling students for that question and answer session would have been better than using hands-up to ensure that all students were engaged in the thinking. However, an impartial observer in the room will spot things that you *didn't* notice yourself, especially if you have agreed a specific shared focus for the observation before you begin. If your professional development focus for the term, or even for the year, is to improve your questioning to extend thinking, then having an observer in the room will sharpen your practice and enable really clear, specific feedback on how you did. Over time, the feedback can be accumulated to identify progress and specific areas for closer work. Just like a coach helping a swimmer to focus on the specific angles of their hands and fingers to ensure maximum purchase in the water, a teacher coach can help to ensure that questions asked have the maximum impact on student learning.

Unfortunately, classroom observation has become tainted over time with the high-stakes accountability system that, for so long, has relied upon snapshot observations to make summative judgments about teacher performance. I have seen this system in operation; I have myself been subject to it in the past. This is the approach to classroom observation in which decisions about teacher performance and, by association, pay progression are made on the basis of observation of a single lesson, graded on a scale of one to four. I'm glad to say that this madness seems to be receding at a national level, helped in no small part by Ofsted's own clarification that they will no longer be grading individual lessons. However, the experience of observation has, for too many teachers, become a threatening and stressful experience. Even when schools have moved away from grading individual lessons, some teachers are still looking for the grade hidden in the feedback, because the observer is still making a judgment about the quality of the lesson. And due to the investment of the self in the profession, mentioned earlier, a judgment about the quality of the lesson very easily becomes a judgment about the quality of the teacher, either in the observer's mind or the teacher's. This judgmental, accountability-driven observation culture pins a judgment to a specific experience at a specific moment in time, fixes it, and creates all manner of perverse incentives to put on special "observation lessons" which bear no resemblance to normal practice and do nothing at all to improve the quality of teaching overall.

Instead, observation needs to be driven by the teacher being observed. The observer should ask the teacher, "what would you like me to focus on that will best help you to improve?" and the observation should then follow that thread through the lesson and, if necessary, beyond and into the work that the students produce subsequently in order to see whether the teaching had any impact on the outcomes. The observer should be subservient to the observed, working to help the teacher to improve, assessing them formatively, not summatively. Above all, the fear factor so often associated with observation needs to be removed so that having someone observe your lesson should be welcomed as an opportunity to get helpful feedback.

Using classroom observation as part of an ongoing coaching programme is the best way to remove that fear factor. The coaching relationship is not hierarchical. Anybody can coach anybody else. In his book *The Best Job in the World*, Vic Goddard describes how he was coached by one of his school's learning support assistants. He tells of the moment he asked her to be his coach: "after she'd picked herself up off the floor, she asked the obvious question, 'What do I know about your job?'"[10] Goddard goes on to show that in coaching, domain knowledge is irrelevant. The process is about helping the colleague being coached to find their own solutions to the issues they are facing. Coaching is a structured professional conversation that will help you make improvements or see opportunities. The coach guides the teacher through a process, following a pattern, but the teacher being coached is in charge: it is about them and what they want.

Of course, the coach won't be there all the time, and this is where the deliberate practice really kicks in. With teachers in a culture of growth, the focus on the developmental priority identified through the coaching relationship will persist even when there is no one watching. When teachers are reflecting either during or immediately after the lesson on how well they delivered as a professional, and how they can continue to improve in their next lesson, then we can begin to say that we have a continuous professional development environment – not just five days a year, but every day.

Swimming against the tide

Building a growth mindset culture for staff development requires school leaders to swim against the prevailing tide of England's accountability culture. For as long as I've been teaching, lesson observation has been associated more with scrutiny and judgment than development and self-improvement. I do think that an element of this is inevitable; whenever you are observed by your line manager, a senior leader, headteacher, colleague, or inspector, there is always going to be an element of wanting to impress them, of wanting to show yourself and your class at their pedagogical best, of wanting to get the validation of being told you are doing a good job. This can lead to covering up deficiencies or concerns, reluctance to take risks, and inaccuracy in the judgments made in the first place. This is amplified in a culture where decisions about a teacher's pay progression depend upon their performance in a single hour's observed lesson and the grade that the observer decides to give them on that day. When thousands of pounds depend on that single-lesson performance, you are unlikely to see it as a developmental opportunity.

At the root of this issue is the question of the purpose of lesson observation. For too long schools have laboured under the misapprehension that sitting in the back of someone's classroom enables the observer to evaluate the quality of teaching and learning that is being delivered. It is certainly not the case that judgments can be formed about the quality of teaching and learning over time within a single lesson observation; I would argue that it is actually impossible to assess accurately the quality of teaching and learning even within that lesson. You might see what looks like high-quality teaching and learning: a well-planned sequence of activities; students engaged and on-task; well-presented and marked books with evidence of improvements made; warm and positive relationships; slick and orderly routines. You might even comment on the quality of classroom display and the learning environment. But to quantify whether what you saw in that lesson actually constitutes high-quality teaching and learning requires a raft of additional triangulating evidence: How successful are the students at recalling what they learned in that lesson three months later? How well embedded are the skills that they were practising? How successful are they in their final assessments? How much progress have they made over time?

I think the prevailing system has put the cart before the horse. In the end, judgments about the quality of teaching and learning can be made on the basis of student outcomes. If they are successful in their assessments, then we can assume they have learned the stuff they have been taught. This evaluation does not require someone sitting in the back of the class. We have, so far, sat in classrooms and seen what we *thought* might be high-quality teaching and learning, and then used assessment data to validate our thinking. I have certainly been in the opposite position of observing what *looked* like high-quality teaching and learning, only to be surprised when the assessment results did not support that judgment. All the fizzy, energetic, coloured-paper, and discovery activities looked great but, in the end, did not lead to the students securely learning what they were being taught.

I suggest, then, that we need to flip this system. Assessment outcomes will tell us where in our schools the most effective teaching and learning is taking place. Lesson observation should then follow that trail and look to find out *how* those teachers are delivering those results. This is the methodology used by Doug Lemov in his Teach Like a Champion[11] resources from the United States. He codified what he found into sixty two techniques used by the most effective teachers, providing an invaluable how-to guide for professionals on either side of the Atlantic. In our own schools, lesson observation can serve the same purpose, but if this is to be effective, then it should not be senior leaders doing the observing. It is counter-intuitive that those who teach least should have the privilege of observing most. Rather, colleagues should be observing to learn from one another and to support and develop their own practice. Colleagues being observed should benefit from the coaching which follows, and observer colleagues should gain from developing their own practice by learning from a fellow professional.

Flipping the observation culture in this way means unlearning the prevailing model, not just for senior leaders but for teachers too. It requires the kind of trust leadership that I referred to in Chapter 6, where senior leaders use assessment data to check on progress and trust that professionals are doing a professional job. Leaders then need to resist the instinctive response to use lesson observations or learning walks to "check up on" people and, instead, use them as genuine fact-finding vehicles to identify *how* great teachers are getting great results, with the aim of codifying and systematising those techniques. Because only when teachers trust that the colleague in their room is not forming judgments about them upon which their pay, their self-esteem, and their professional reputation depend will they be open to the constructive, formative feedback that the coaching relationship can provide.

How we did it

In his keynote address to the SSAT National Conference in 2012, Dylan Wiliam spoke with his usual eloquence about the need to improve teacher quality in order to prepare our students for a world we cannot possibly imagine.[12] It was in this address that he said, almost as a throwaway remark at the end: "every teacher needs to improve, not because they are not good enough, but because they can be even better." Wiliam's quote has since become totemic for many teachers and school leaders as a driver for good-quality professional development. When we undertook the redevelopment of our school's approach and ethos in order to become a growth mindset school, we recognised the need to reorganise our approach to professional development too, instituting an approach of deliberate practice and peer coaching across the school. The approach that I now advocate is using Teaching and Learning Leaders appointed from within the existing staff body.

The idea had first begun to percolate when I went to Keven Bartle's workshop at a TeachMeet held at Clevedon School in October 2012, a couple of months before Dylan Wiliam's address to the conference. In his session, Keven outlined his model of bottom-up CPD run by classroom teachers, his antidote to the top-down model that had become anathema to me over many Inset days spent listening to another expensive speaker who had been brought in to support development but who would provide no lasting impact on my practice. It made perfect sense to me, and Kev continued to evangelise the "pedagogy leaders" model in a *Guardian* article in June. The principle is described as follows:

> an approach to the development of teaching and learning . . . that doesn't come top-down from a member of the senior leadership team with an "amazing idea" but instead emerges from the experiences and insights of those true classroom-heroes who teach four out of five periods every day. [13]

I jumped at the opportunity to visit Canons High in December 2013 to hear how they had approached the project and to hear and see the pedagogy leaders in action. It was hugely impressive. The pedagogy leaders not only worked to develop the quality of teaching across the school, but also worked as a team to drive improvement in teaching and learning across the whole school. The school had the data and the external validation to back it up. Needless to say I was absolutely convinced that this model worked – and that it could work for us. We adapted the pedagogy leaders model to our own context, creating the idea of Teaching and Learning Leaders.

Crucial to the concept was that it should involve all staff. In September, every teacher joins a cross-curricular Teaching and Learning Team. In the first iteration of the programme, the Teaching and Learning Teams focused on developing a growth mindset through:

- Differentiation
- Marking and Feedback
- Questioning
- Literacy and Numeracy
- Independent learning

However, the specialisms of these teams has diversified considerably as the programme has developed and according to the need of the particular context. Each team was headed up by a Teaching and Learning Leader, and I have run different models for this. Initially I made the role a paid responsibility, but actually time to observe practice, work with colleagues, provide coaching, and identify best practice in their expertise area is just as valuable for the Teaching and Learning Leaders. Also, just as importantly, Teaching & Learning Leaders were entitled to (and expected to use) a full day to visit other schools to find best practice in their specialist area. This could be split to allow visits to more than one school. The posts would be held for one academic year and new Teaching and Learning Leaders would be appointed in the following year, although there was nothing to stop existing postholders from reapplying.

Once appointed, the Teaching and Learning Leaders were given a professional development programme themselves, covering the key aspects of the role. This included:

- Developing growth mindset

- Leadership skills

- Coaching

- Lesson observation

- Facilitation

- Sharing best practice

These sessions were crucial for the Teaching and Learning Leaders in shaping their vision for the programme and deciding on their priorities. It was important, as outlined in Chapter 6, that these staff were trusted to lead and develop the programme autonomously, although with support provided if needed.

The advantages of the Teaching and Learning Teams approach were manifold. It embodied the values of distributed leadership that stem from a trust culture, and it valued the practice of teachers who worked at the chalkface. The teams systematised cross-curricular working which can – especially in large secondary schools – fall by the wayside as teachers function in their separate subject-specific silos. Having a year-long project and team membership ensured that the whole staff had a regular and continuous focus on key teaching and learning issues, where they were working collaboratively to improve their practice and pushing their own teaching and learning forward. It also implemented the coaching model, as Teaching and Learning Leaders (and, indeed, team members themselves) would observe one another teach in order to provide helpful developmental feedback rather than evaluative judgments. And finally, being a Teaching and Learning Leader provided a really positive opportunity for leadership experience and professional development for teachers who didn't necessarily want to move away from the classroom and into curriculum or pastoral roles in the school, focusing skilful professionals on improving practice not just for themselves but for others by developing expertise in a specific area.

I have used a similar approach ever since, both at Chew Valley and then at Churchill. Having staff lead in an area of pedagogy in which they are interested empowers them and works to drive reflection and improvement across the school, being fed by and simultaneously feeding a growth mindset culture. Rather than being owned by the guru brought in from outside for a morning on an Inset day, where all visit to drink at the waterhole of knowledge before being returned to their barren classrooms, the teaching and learning team approach leads to a fertile environment across the school. Because conversations about teaching and learning are being had across the school, all the time, it is hard to track and pin down. It might seem that we aren't "doing" professional development, because there are a smaller number of high-profile events. But actually the paradigm has shifted from single high-profile but low-impact events to countless low-profile but high-impact ones. The peer-to-peer coaching conversation based on a lesson that two professionals have both just been in, focusing on a specific area of practice that the colleagues have been researching and practising all year, will make far more difference than any shiny ring-binder or colourful Inset day presentation – and the evidence will be in the students' results.

Conclusion

For teachers to avoid the plateau effect identified by Rivkin, Hanushek, and Kain, the need for continuous improvement is a necessity. Charles Handy characterises this in *The Empty Raincoat*: "what got you where you are won't keep you where you are."[14] This continuous improvement, in turn, requires growth mindset thinking. It needs teachers to receive and act on critique, learning from the example of others in order to develop and grow. It therefore needs a culture where professional development is the constant thread in the work of schools, with reflective practice taking place in classrooms and conversations on a daily basis, not just on flip-chart paper on an Inset day twice or three times a year. It means that the norm for observers visiting classrooms is developmental, not judgmental. And it means that for all teachers, their focus in the classroom should be the same as that of their students: "how can I get better at this today than I was yesterday?"

Notes

1 This plateau effect was documented by Rivkin, Hanushek, & Kain, "Teachers, schools and academic achievement."
2 TDA/CUREE (*Evaluation of CPD Providers in England 2010–11*) show that only 1 per cent of CPD provision was rated as "transformative" to teaching practice.
3 Matthew Hood presented his ideas as part of Radio 4's *Four Thought* strand in a programme called "Performance teaching."

4 Ericsson, Krampe, & Tesch-Romer, "The role of deliberate practice in the acquisition of expert performance."
5 Ibid., page 400.
6 Gladwell, *Outliers.*
7 Syed, *Bounce.*
8 Duckworth, *Grit.*
9 Ibid., page 135.
10 Goddard, *The Best Job in the World*, page 122.
11 See Lemov, *Teach Like a Champion 2.0.*
12 Wiliam, "How do we prepare our students" – the address can still be seen on *YouTube*: https://youtu.be/r1LL9NX1hUw
13 Bartle, "The pedagogy leaders project."
14 Handy, *The Empty Raincoat*, page 58.

Bibliography

Bartle, K. (2014, 14 June). The pedagogy leaders project: How our staff drive teaching and learning. Retrieved 5 March, 2017, from The Guardian Education Blog: https://www.theguardian.com/teacher-network/teacher-blog/2013/jun/14/pedagogy-staff-initiative-teaching-learning-project

Duckworth, A. (2016). *Grit.* London: Vermilion.

Ericsson, K. A., Krampe, R., & Tesch-Romer, C. (1993). The role of deliberate practice in the acquisition of expert performance. *Psychological Review, 100*(3), 363–406.

Faulkner, W. (1956). The art of fiction. (J. Stein, Interviewer), *The Paris Review.*

Gladwell, M. (2009). *Outliers.* London: Penguin.

Goddard, V. (2014). *The Best Job in the World.* Carmarthen: Crown House Publishing.

Handy, C. (1995). *The Empty Raincoat.* London: Random House.

Hood, M. (2016, 21 December). Performance teaching. *Four Thought.* BBC Radio Four.

Lemov, D. (2015). *Teach Like a Champion 2.0.* San Francisco: Jossey Bass.

Macnamara, B. N., Hambrick, D. Z., & Oswald, F. L. (2014). Deliberate practice and performance in music, games, sports, education and professions: A meta-analysis. *Psychological Science, 25*(8), 1608–1618.

O'Leary, M. (2013). *Classroom Observation: A Guide to the Effective Observation of Teaching and Learning.* London: Routledge.

Rivkin, S. G., Hanushek, E. A., & Kain, J. F. (2005, March). Teachers, schools and academic achievement. *Econometrica, 73*(2), 417–458.

Syed, M. (2011). *Bounce.* London: Fourth Estate.

TDA/CUREE. (2011). *Evaluation of CPD Providers in England 2010–11.* Coventry, UK: Centre for the Use of Research and Evidence in Education.

Wiliam, D. (2012, 5 December). How do we prepare our students for a world we cannot possibly imagine? Keynote address: *SSAT National Conference*, Liverpool.

12 Growth mindset for students and families

Children spend around 1,300 hours in school over the course of a year[1] – just over 15 per cent of their time. If they get a regular eight hours of sleep each night, that totals up to 2,920 hours unconscious, leaving over 4,500 hours outside of school time in an average year. Attempts by a school to influence and adjust attitudes to and beliefs about learning in its students will have some effect – the time spent in school is not insignificant – but a partnership between home and school is essential if these attitudes and approaches are going to be reinforced and supported rather than undermined and weakened. In this chapter, I will explore the ways in which we have worked with students and their families to extend the growth mindset ethos beyond the influence of the school staff, giving it a life of its own within the student body and out into the community.

Spheres of influence

Teachers cannot control everything within a school. A teacher has complete control (we would hope) of their own behaviour, language, tone, resources, and material. In the delivery of that material and in their interactions with students, they have a direct influence on the way those students learn and behave. Beyond that, there is only an indirect influence (see Figure 12.1). The hope is that the influence teachers have had on learning and behaviour within the classroom will extend out indirectly to student behaviours in their wider learning and life beyond those lessons, seeping into the fabric of their lives and helping them to be more effective, self-determined, and confident young people. In our moments of strongest idealism, we hope that these influences will have a knock-on effect to "everything," building a more coherent and positive society with equity and equality for all. But the actual direct control we have over those things is limited, and in complex systems like schools and wider societies, our influences can sometimes have unexpected and unintended consequences.

Letting go of that "control" has been a hard but necessary lesson for me as I have moved into school leadership. I have always liked the simple formula: do x, and y

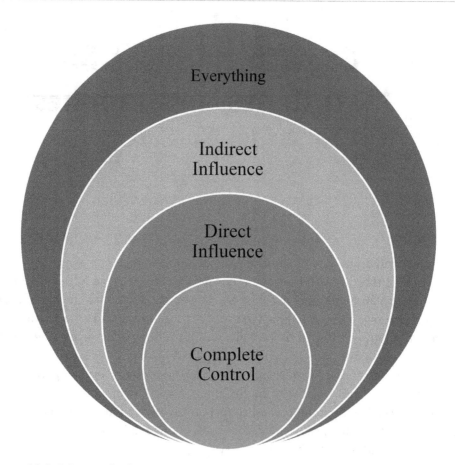

Figure 12.1 Spheres of influence

happens as a result. Teach the students this material today, and they will remember it tomorrow. Explain to them how the brain learns new material by forming and strengthening neural pathways, and surely they will understand and adopt the growth mindset. Would that it were so simple! As I explained in Chapter 6, leadership is a much more complex process, and leaders in schools (meaning both the designated school leadership teams and the teachers leading learning in their own classrooms) need to become comfortable with the fact that their direct influence only extends so far. In building an ethos and a culture which promotes a growth mindset, it had been important for us to use the interventions over which we had complete control to directly influence the school environment but also, where possible, family understanding and support for our approach and the work of primary schools which worked with us. At the same time, we hoped to create a "ripple effect" where the culture over which we had a direct influence would push outwards to influence the wider community and beyond.

The importance of family support for school culture was highlighted by a student who I will call "Jade." Jade was a delightful young woman – hard-working, well behaved, and conscientious – but she was not achieving her potential in GCSE Maths. At the start of Year 11 she was predicted an E grade, but needed a C to progress to A-levels in the sixth form (her preferred destination). We called Jade in with her mother for an interview to discuss what we could do to rectify the situation. "What's happening with this Maths grade, Jade?" Jade was resigned to the situation: "I've never been any good at maths, Sir. It just never clicks with me." Jade's mum put her arm round her daughter and said, "it's alright, Jade, I was never any good at maths either." The gesture was well intentioned, aimed at rescuing Jade's self-esteem, but in that one statement Jade had her low attainment in Maths condoned and accepted. The chances of convincing Jade that she could, in fact, "do maths," dwindled in that instance to something approaching zero. She continued to work hard throughout Year 11, attended extra sessions, and did as much revision as she could, but she went on to get her predicted E.

I very rarely meet families who don't want the best possible outcomes for their children. Certainly, some families place more value on schoolwork than others, but the overwhelming majority would move heaven and earth for their children. But although they want to help, they don't necessarily know *how* to help; they are not all educationalists or psychologists. Our work in schools has to help families focus that energy in the most productive and significant directions. In the health service, trained experts provide help and guidance to parents to ensure that children have healthy diets and lifestyles and that they are vaccinated against major diseases. Teachers are the trained experts in the education system, so it is our role to help families support children in the most effective learning approaches.

Reaching out to families

We take every opportunity to reach out to families and help them to understand the ethos of the school and how they can support that at home. The prime opportunity to do this in a secondary school is on transition, when the children first start with us. This is the time when families are most focused on education, keen to be involved and to get it right, especially with the eldest child. It's also the time when you get the most families engaged with the school, attending information evenings and meeting key staff. This is the time, therefore, when we need to get it right.

At our transition evening, we explain the basics of mindset theory and the supporting neuroscience. We use a similar approach to the staff launch, described in Chapter 5, with a mixture of video presentation and explanation aimed at helping families understand how they can help. It's important not to overload this session as parents have a lot to take in on events like this – the child's tutor, the house they're in, the names of the friends they've met on the transition day, the times of the school day, the uniform expectations, which bus their child is going to catch, what they'll need for PE, how to pay for school dinners . . . these practical aspects of schooling take a high priority in the minds of many anxious families. But, as Headteacher, it's my role to emphasise the primary purpose of them coming to school in the first place: learning. Therefore we lead with this in my presentation to parents, and I give them three simple pieces of advice:

1. Praise the process

2. Seek out difficulty

3. Use the power of "yet"

The first piece of advice is simple. I run through Mueller and Dweck's study[2] of how praise for intelligence can undermine motivation and performance by fixing mindsets, and I provide a few simple alternatives to intelligence praise for the parents to use: "well done, you must have tried really hard at that!" is the classic from the study, but "that's great – can you tell me how you got there?" is more helpful in this context as it provokes a conversation around strategies, techniques, and approaches, showing the child that the parents' interest is not so much in the product as the process. Similarly, providing families with simple alternatives to encourage them to praise the process, not the person, can be helpful. So, instead of saying "you're so good at English/Art/Science," try "you've really pushed yourself on this project – it's great to see you working so hard at it." Instead of "you're so clever/brilliant/wonderful," try "I'm so proud of the way you've put your time and energy into this" or "we're so happy to see that you persevered with this – it was worth all that effort, wasn't it?" Initially, I was worried about patronising parents with this kind of presentation, but in fact I've never had a bad reaction to it.[3] On the contrary, families are grateful for concrete advice and guidance, and keen to do the best by their children.

The second piece of advice is, predictably perhaps, more difficult. There is something counter-intuitive about it for parents, who instinctively rush to praise when children "get" something quickly or produce perfect work first time. The key message here, however, is that learning is the product of struggle. If students find something quick and easy to grasp, the likelihood is that they either knew it (or something very like it) already or the level of challenge was too low. Instead, we only semi-jokingly invoke Dweck's fantasy dinner-table conversation: "who had a fabulous struggle today?" Or, when children get something quickly and easily: "oh, sorry to have wasted your time. Let's find something challenging, something you can learn from."[4] More seriously, we urge families to praise struggle and to seek out challenging tasks for their children to do and challenging texts for them to read, to reinforce the message that we give in school: if you're finding it easy, you're not learning anything; if you're struggling, you're learning.

Finally, we provide families with the abracadabra of mindset – the magic word "yet." We talk about how "yet" can help when students fail or when they are in the midst of the struggle to master a new and challenging concept. "I can't do it" or "I'll never get it" or "I've never been able to do this" – these statements can all be turned around with ". . . yet." Learning is a process, and students are always on an upward curve. If they can't do it today, they'll have to try again tomorrow, perhaps coming at it from a different angle or using a different strategy. I talk to them about Jade and her mother, and I tell them how damaging such well-intentioned platitudes can be. If a parent struggled with maths or languages or spelling at school, by all means share that struggle with your child; but share it with the understanding that the child will be able to conquer it if they apply themselves and get the help and support they need – giving up is not an option.

Once these seeds have been planted at the start of school, the messages are reinforced in every future interaction. We hold curriculum information evenings annually for each year group in the school, outlining the programmes of study and key pastoral information (including a great session on the physical, emotional, and hormonal changes parents can expect as Year 8 children go into Year 9), and we reiterate the three key messages: praise the process; seek out difficulty; use the power of "yet." In parents' evenings, the annual tour of each class teacher, staff provide focused feedback on the attitude and approach that students have to their learning, as well as their progress through the content, emphasising the strategies that students have used and modelling process praise to remind parents of the emphasis. At options evening at the transition to the next key stage, I always emphasise that students are opting for subjects that they will take for the duration of the course: there is no dropping out. Taking an option is a commitment, and resilience, grit, and determination are required to stick it out to the end. Our guide for families to support student revision,[5] aimed at those in Year 11 and the sixth form, is based on proven techniques from neuro-scientific research, and it emphasises the importance of struggle and difficulty to securing knowledge in the memory. And at prize-giving, our "celebration of success" awards, we recognise those students whose attitudes to learning have led to the greatest achievement and progress, and praise them for their strategies and approaches, and their perseverance, determination, effort, and hard work. At every turn we communicate to parents that these are the things we value; these are the things that are important to us; this is what matters.

Inevitably, the families that turn up to all these events are the most engaged and supportive, and generally the ones whose children need help least. I don't have any silver bullets for engaging "hard-to-reach" families; we do the usual things like coffee mornings, phone calls, and home visits, and we use electronic communication via text messaging, email, and increasingly social media to connect with as many families as possible. I write a weekly blog, which is a mixture of good news stories from the life of the school, growth mindset examples, and learning strategy advice.[6] And those engaged, supportive families that turn up to everything are often just as much in need of support as the hard-to-reach families, and they have always (in my experience) been grateful for advice and guidance, keen to implement the strategies that we are using in school so that the messages are reinforced at home. There is a risk, I think, of assuming that just because families are supportive of school and turn up to things, they automatically have the expertise they need. Of course we should reach out to the hard-to-reach families, but working with the coalition of the willing should not be ignored. Bolstering those areas where we are already strong can be a powerful surplus model. The same is true of primary school, where often the relationship with families is even closer than at secondary.

Working across phases

As Headteacher of a secondary school, I have found that many of the young people arrive with pre-existing mindsets from their experience at primary. Working closely with colleagues from the primary sector is imperative so that the formative years of education, from Reception class upwards, emphasise the same approaches. Although I am a secondary school teacher and all of my experience to date has been in secondary schools, the approaches that I have explained in this book apply equally to primary as they do to secondary. This does not mean telling primary colleagues how we want things done; in my experience, secondary teachers have more to learn from primary than the other way around. It simply means joining up and matching our approaches so that we value the same things and so that the students benefit from consistency in terms of the values and vision for education that they experience throughout their schooling.

Multi-academy trusts, federations, and other collaborative structures have proliferated in England since 2010, and this trend seems set to continue. This is not the place for a detailed analysis of the academies initiative, but what multi-academy trusts do allow is an agreement of shared vision and values between schools in a formal collaboration. Indeed, for them to be successful, this is not just permitted but required.[7] This means, in my view, they provide significant opportunity for explicitly shared approaches across the age range and the kind of coherence that schools working in the same authorities or even in looser collaborative structures (such as clusters) lack. The same advantages apply across multiple schools as apply in a single-school context: mindset theory doesn't dictate a particular teaching style or method, it doesn't dictate a specific curriculum, it doesn't mandate particular approaches to grouping or differentiation or the colour of pen you mark in or the seating arrangements in your classroom. What it does do is call for all the schools within the collaboration to agree that intelligence and ability are not fixed, but can grow with effort and application, and to approach each teaching and learning decision informed by that agreement. How a trust or federation formulates its vision around that core is absolutely up to the local context, the circumstances of the schools, and the needs of their students.

Within the primary context, the possibilities to apply this in practice are legion. At one school's weekly celebration assembly, alongside the headteacher's "Magic Moments" and the awarding of the House Trophy, they have a "mistakes are great, they help us learn" slot, where children are invited to share a great mistake they made during the week and how it helped them to make progress. I love this approach; what I love even more is the forest of hands which goes up in the hall in front of peers, teachers, and parents, arms strained almost out of their sockets as children are desperate for *their* mistake to be chosen this week: "I was doing two-digit addition and subtraction," said one Year 3 student, "and I added instead of subtracting." The headteacher smiled. "That's great," he said, "and what did you learn from that mistake?" "That I always need to look at the operator," said the student.

This kind of public celebration of error is nuanced. The teachers are careful *only* to celebrate the mistakes which led to learning. The sophistication of the Year 3 student's response to the follow up was what made that exchange for me, with the use of technical language embedded in the answer and the sense that the experience of error was a formative one. And this happens every single week at this school, normalising and foregrounding the necessity of struggle and the inevitability of error when taking on hard tasks and learning from them. Similarly teachers in primary classrooms might use "mistake of the day" awards, or they might encourage effort-based self-talk in feedback. Jo Payne, a Year 4 teacher, uses soft-toy characters to personify (or anthropomorphise) the mindsets into "Really Hard Ratty" and "Work-at-it Wiz" (a rat and a hare – just because!) to allow younger children to identify the approaches they are taking to their work. Are they being a "Wiz" with their lessons?[8]

What is clear is that getting mindset right requires joined-up thinking from across the educational continuum. Providing that the institutions have connected their approaches, effective learning habits established early can be maintained through transitions. When these effective learning habits are understood and supported by families in the communities around their schools, the impact is amplified. But to truly embed a growth mindset, the concept and the culture needs to be owned by the students themselves.

Student leadership: growth mindset ambassadors

Graham Nuthall spent forty years researching learning and teaching. His method – using an array of cameras and microphones within his classroom, collecting every single thing that children wrote in class, and interviewing the participants afterwards – gave him and his team an absolute mass of data for analysis to try to understand what was happening in lessons. Towards the end of his life, he collected his thoughts about what he had discovered in *The Hidden Lives of Learners*,[9] a must-read for any educator. Amongst his findings was the fact that every student sitting within the same lesson learned differently, dependent on their prior experience, knowledge, and disposition. The link between what was taught by the teacher and what was learned by the students was tenuous at best; at least, what the teacher intended the students to learn was not what they actually learned. In particular, he showed how one student's misunderstanding of what the teacher meant can easily spread through several other students in the class, resulting in a mis-learning effect.

Nuthall characterises three separate cultural spheres in operation in the classroom (or the school). These are linked to the spheres of influence I mentioned earlier. The first, the public sphere, is controlled by the teacher. This is the one that we know about, where we can exert our influence; this is the sphere that we want the students to buy in to, to be engaged and motivated by, and to pay attention to. However, sitting underneath the public sphere is the private social sphere of the students, which is far more influential than perhaps we give it credit for. This is the sphere in which peer influence operates and the distractions and hierarchies of the children's lives are played out – the events which occur "under the surface" of the school and which even the most astute teachers see only a fraction of. Nuthall contends that it is this sphere which is the dominant one for student learning in the classroom, rather than the public sphere of the teacher, and that learning is much more influenced by the private peer culture than it is by the lesson plan and input from the member of staff at the front of the room.

The third sphere is the inner world of each individual student themselves. Whilst Nuthall was able to gather copious evidence of the students' private social sphere through his hidden cameras and microphones, he (perhaps) accessed more aspects of individual students' inner worlds through interviews. This inner world is necessarily mysterious, enigmatic, and truly hidden. Importantly, it is in this hidden inner world where the learner's mindset resides. Their own beliefs about their own ability and intelligence sit inside their minds, and we can never truly know what they are thinking. Whilst they might answer a questionnaire to indicate that they "strongly agree" with the statement "you can substantially change how intelligent you are," there may be a raft of different reasons for this response, ranging from wanting to have a particular score, wanting to be seen in a different way, wanting to convince themselves that this is really what they believe, and so on. We can never really know. But what we do know, from our own experiences, is that we can change our minds about things. When presented with enough evidence or when the influence is significant enough, our beliefs can and do shift from one position to another. As adults, we are familiar with this happening inside our own minds, and whilst we can never truly know whether the shift has happened in the mind of another, we can attempt to influence a change.

What Nuthall contends is that the influence of the private social sphere of students is more significant in influencing their behaviour, learning, and approach than the public world of the teacher. This means that if we are going to root the growth mindset in the ethos of a school, teachers providing process-based feedback and praise for effort are only going to get us so far. If we want it to work, the student culture has to adopt the growth mindset too. I know that this can be transformational. One school I know of saw a 10 per cent jump in GCSE attainment three years ago, with a set of headline figures which made them the envy of the local education community. The deputy head there was, naturally, asked to share the secret of the school's success with colleagues in the next network meeting for senior leaders. "It wasn't really anything we did differently," he explained.

At the start of Year 11, a group of about ten boys, all in the rugby team, came back and collectively decided they were going to work really hard. They were popular boys, and they just took the rest of the year group with them.

Underpinning his explanation is the impact of the students' private social sphere. It's what Kellan experienced as she sat in the sixth form study centre and saw her peers working hard and making lots of notes. When you see everybody else doing something, that's what you do too. If schools can achieve a critical mass of students adopting a growth mindset, then the culture will effectively take care of itself.

This idea was adopted by Rebecca Tushingham at another local school, as detailed on her blog, Growth Mindset Journey.[10] She recruited a group of growth mindset ambassadors from within the student body to spread the word amongst their peers and to model the approach for others. They also presented to staff as part of a training event, truly demonstrating that they were deserving of their title by taking on this challenge and pushing themselves. Of the initial group of nine, five went on to apply to be House Captains, and "the general consensus was that having presented at an INSET to all of their teachers last summer being a student leader in a different context didn't seem impossible."[11] Using student leaders allows ownership of mindset theory within the student body and offsets the risks of top-down, teacher-led "nagging" approaches.

Inspired by the "ambassadors" programme, we have adopted a similar strategy. However, rather than branding them with a "growth mindset ambassador" badge, we have taken a more stealthy approach, working with a group of students to explain the principles of growth mindset and then allowing them to devise their own plans for seeding the mindset amongst the student body. They have trialled a number of different projects over the course of their first year, including a trial peer-mentoring programme and a series of student-led activities through tutor time. Their mission statement (which they wrote themselves) was:

> We want to represent the message of "people becoming inspired to learn." Students should be taking responsibilities for learning, to become self-motivated to be independent about their own learning. This would mean the stopping of afterschool revision classes. This will allow students to become driven and empowered to learn.

Shifting the critical mass of the student body is an inexact science. Within our own classes, we might identify influential students and work closely with them, shifting their behaviour and attitude and letting that ripple out to the rest of the student body. We already "divide and rule" by splitting up unproductive pairings in our seating plans; what I am proposing is to flip this and scale it up. Focus on the students who are the normative influence in the class, the year group, or the school: are they demonstrating the value of effort, of taking on hard challenges, of learning from critique and error, of struggle and difficulty? If they are, how can we amplify that culture, giving them a voice to spread the word? If they aren't, what influence can we exert to shift their attitudes and behaviour? What responsibility can we give them? How can we engage them in the process so they do the work of spreading that approach more widely through their peer group? The answers to those questions will be different in every school, but if you can get those students into leadership roles, they will act as Trojan Horses for the growth mindset and – if Graham Nuthall is right – have a far greater influence than any number of inspirational assemblies.

Notes

1 Assuming a school day from 8:30 a.m. to 3:30 p.m. over 190 taught days in the school year.
2 Mueller & Dweck, "Praise for intelligence can undermine children's motivation and performance."
3 . . . yet.
4 From Dweck's RSA speech, "How to help every child fulfil their potential."
5 This guide is available to download here: https://churchillhead.files.wordpress.com/2016/01/helping-your-child-revise-2016.pdf
6 The Headteacher's Blog can be found at: https://churchillhead.com/
7 Sir David Carter notes this in good practice guidance for multi-academy trusts.
8 You can read more about Jo Payne's work on her blog, Mrs P Teach.
9 Nuthall, *The Hidden Lives of Learners*.
10 You can read Rebecca's blog at: https://growthmindsetjourney.blogspot.co.uk/
11 From Tushingham's blog: "Student leadership will provide the change we're looking for."

Bibliography

Carter, D. (2016, December). Multi-academy trusts: Good practice guidance and expectations for growth. Retrieved 21 April, 2017, from *GOV.UK*: https://www.gov.uk/government/publications/multi-academy-trusts-establishing-and-developing-your-trust

Dweck, C. (2015, 15 December). How to help every child fulfil their potential. Retrieved 23 December, 2016, from *The RSA*: https://www.thersa.org/discover/videos/rsa-animate/2015/how-to-help-every-child-fulfil-their-potential

Mueller, C. M., & Dweck, C. S. (1998). Praise for intelligence can undermine children's motivation and performance. *Journal of Personality and Social Psychology, 75*(1), 33–52.

Nuthall, G. (2007). *The Hidden Lives of Learners*. Wellington: NZCER Press.

Payne, J. (2015, 9 February). Growth mindset in my primary classroom. Retrieved 21 April, 2017, from *Mrs P Teach*: www.mrspteach.com/2015/02/growth-mindset-in-my-primary-classroom.html

Tushingham, R. (2014, 7 December). Student leadership will provide the change we're looking for. Retrieved 21 April, 2017, from *Growth Mindset Journey*: https://growthmindsetjourney.blogspot.co.uk/2014/12/student-leadership-will-provide-change.html

Zander, B. (2006, 10 July). Benjamin Zander: Gurus. Retrieved 10 April, 2017, from *TeachFind*: http://archive.teachfind.com/ttv/www.teachers.tv/videos/benjamin-zander.html

13 Growth mindset misconceptions and missteps

Over the course of trying to build a growth mindset ethos, I have found repeated misconceptions about the approach. It's also not a static field: research into the psychology of motivation and learning is constantly developing, and therefore advances and revisions to the science are happening all the time. This chapter considers the difficulties in understanding and implementation of the growth mindset, ending with an outline of the strategies that we have found to be the most – and the least – effective in becoming a growth mindset school.

Is growth mindset research even valid?

As interest in mindset research has grown on both sides of the Atlantic, researchers have been trying to find the approaches which will have the most significant impact on student grades. Much of this research has been useful, suggesting tweaks to Dweck's recommendations from laboratory study with promising results in "live" classroom environments. However, this has not always been the case, as shown in a 2017 paper from Edinburgh University titled *Does growth mindset improve children's IQ, educational attainment or response to setbacks?* Li and Bates "found no support for mindset-effects on cognitive ability, response to challenge, or educational progress."[1] Across their sample size of 624 in three separate replication attempts, their findings cast doubt on the validity of mindset as a significant factor in student achievement and attainment.

Similarly, the Education Endowment Foundation tested mindset interventions in a 2015 study,[2] using a randomised control trial with 286 children across six schools. On average, students who received growth mindset interventions made two additional months' progress in both English and Maths compared to those who had received the control intervention (study skills). However, this gain was not statistically significant – it is possible that it could have been down to chance. The study was also compromised as some of the teachers involved in the trial were already aware of the concept of growth and fixed mindset and, therefore, may already have been using the approaches in their classrooms: "previous exposure to the approach may have weakened the relative impact of the intervention."[3]

On top of this, the relative malleability of intelligence and the significance of heritability and genetics continue to be a source of debate. Dominic Cummings, special advisor to Secretary of State for Education Michael Gove between 2010 and 2014, outlined his contention that the role of genetics in student attainment is more significant than widespread opinion would have it:

> there is such strong resistance across the political spectrum to accepting scientific evidence on genetics. . . . Most of those that now dominate discussions on issues such as "social mobility" entirely ignore genetics and therefore their arguments are at best misleading and often worthless.[4]

Cummings' claimed that research showed as much as 70 per cent of a child's performance is genetically derived, citing the work of Robert Plomin and others.

Plomin is himself a fascinating figure. He was embroiled in the controversy surrounding *The Bell Curve*, a 1994 book by Harvard psychology professor Richard Herrnstein and political scientist Charles Murray, which stated that black people in the United States had an average IQ of 85 against 103 for white people.[5] The argument suggested that this difference was genetic and that once this was taken into account, many racial differences in educational attainment and career achievement were nullified. Plomin defended the science, although he distanced himself from the eugenics conclusions reached by Herrnstein and Murray. His view today is that the differences in IQ between racial and social groups pale into insignificance compared to the variance within those groups.[6] Plomin continues to strive in the field of genetics and education to help people to understand the role that our genes play. In one particularly striking argument, he takes on the idea that a child who grows up in a house filled with books is more likely to be successful in school because of the stimulating environment in which they have been raised. It's far more likely, his argument goes, that this success at school is genetic inheritance and that the house full of books is a marker of parental intelligence and academic ability. In other words, the house full of books is evidence of nature, not an example of nurture. His continuing (and, to date, unsuccessful) mission is to find the genes responsible for determining IQ, and his long-term vision is for an education system where children's innate strengths and weaknesses are encoded onto an individual learning chip so that their curriculum experience can be tailored to their genetic predispositions.

The debates around nature vs nurture in education tend to be polarising. However, the truth of the matter is more nuanced than the binary view which is often presented. Dweck and others within the pro-growth-mindset camp certainly understand the importance of genetics and the "natural ability" we inherit from our family line, although their fundamental emphasis is on changing these abilities through the effort we put in. What is particularly interesting is that Plomin's research (and that of many others in the field) is focused on the heritability of IQ, and he acknowledges that other aspects of our intelligence, aptitude, and ability are much more malleable. The following is an excerpt from an interview with Plomin in 2013:

> "It's not just aptitude that's important in a child," says Plomin. "It's what I call appetite, just for the alliteration. I mean, conscientiousness, which means things like grit and sticking to it." But isn't that genetic too? "So, there's a genetic component to everything, but it's a lot less than IQ."[7]

In this argument, I feel, lies the middle ground in the debate. We are all born with a certain amount of natural ability, but having a growth mindset – and grit, self-control, conscientiousness, and an intellectual "appetite" – will allow us to make the most of what natural ability we inherit.

Carol Dweck herself has responded to the failure to replicate studies in a blog post entitled "Growth mindset is on a firm foundation, but we're still building the house." In a dignified response to the sample sizes of 624 and 286 in the Edinburgh University and Education Endowment Foundation studies, she reminds us that

> A meta-analysis[8] published in 2013 found 113 studies conducted by many authors and concluded that mindsets are a significant factor in people's self-regulation toward goals.
>
> [. . .] Government data collected at a country level—all the 10th grade students in the country of Chile (over 160,000)—showed that holding a growth mindset predicted academic achievement at every socioeconomic level. Recently, the state of California, collecting data from over 100,000 middle schoolers, found that students' mindsets were a good predictor of their test scores.[9]

After thirty years of study and with a wealth of evidence to back it up, it does seem as though Dweck has a compelling case. But with this kind of support for mindset research, why are the findings so hard to replicate? And why aren't the students in our schools suddenly doing so much better after we show them how the brain learns?

Growth mindset pitfalls: understanding and implementation

Dweck's explanation for this is the subtlety and nuance associated with mindset science and the potential for misunderstanding. Indeed, she says,

> We began to see and accumulate research evidence that the growth mindset concept was poorly understood by many parents and educators and that adults might not know how to pass a growth mindset on to children, even when they reported holding it for themselves.[10]

This has certainly been the case with us, as implementing a growth mindset ethos is much more complicated than merely explaining how the brain works and then telling the children to work harder.

Nudge not bludgeon

One misstep I think we took in our launch of a growth mindset ethos at Chew Valley, due in part to the enthusiasm we felt as staff for the project, is that we made too much fuss. We changed the signage up and down the school; we placed inspirational growth mindset quotations along every corridor; we required students to reflect weekly on their learning approaches. It was teacher-led and this ran the risk of creating a condition which we came to recognise as "growth mindset fatigue" – the tendency of teenagers to groan whenever the term was mentioned. In short, by going in all guns blazing, we moved on very quickly from encouraging students to adopt a growth mindset to nagging them to have one. And it doesn't take an Ivy League professor of psychology to tell you that the only guarantee when you nag a teenager into doing something is that they will very quickly start to resist.

The posters we put up around the school – famous faces accompanied by growth mindset quotations – probably had very little impact and most likely encouraged students to resist the interventions as they were too overt. However, as a visible signal of the school's vision and values, they definitely worked. Which leads to the question: if you are putting up a growth mindset display at the back of your classroom or deciding which inspirational quotation to stencil in the corridors of your school, why are you doing this? What do you want the impact to be? And who is it for? The students? Or you? One issue we faced was that we were labelling and badging everything with "growth mindset," whereas it is perfectly possible to promote a belief in incremental self-theory without ever mentioning the term.

Of course, it would be wonderful to think that you could do one big assembly at the start of the year and then suddenly all your students would become growth mindset learners, willing to take on challenges and persist in the face of setbacks. But we know this is not the case. In fact, I discovered this in person when teaching a GCSE Media Studies lesson at Chew Valley. I was trying to persuade a Year 10 student that the magazine cover she was mocking up would be much improved if she moved away from Times New Roman font, the default in the desktop publishing package she was using. The conversation went something like this:

> *Me:* You'll need to go through and work on those fonts and re-edit the picture if you want to improve that.
>
> *Student:* Do I have to?
>
> *Me:* It's the only way you're going to improve it.
>
> *Student:* Yeah, but, you know . . . effort. *sigh* *pout*
>
> *Me:* Effort is what ignites your ability and turns it into accomplishment, you know.
>
> *Student:* Can't I just hand it in like this?

And this was weeks after the big growth mindset assembly. It was at this point I was forced to admit that you can't change someone's mindset for them; they need to change it themselves. No matter how powerful mindset interventions might be, they are not a silver bullet that will suddenly resolve all learning issues in one fell swoop.

David Yeager and Gregory Walton clearly understood this issue when they penned their cautionary paper "Social-Psychological Interventions in Education: They're Not Magic."[11] Looking into the research in detail, Yeager and Walton make it clear that interventions are effective when they "target students' subjective experiences in school, . . . [when] they use persuasive yet stealthy methods for conveying psychological ideas, and [when] they tap into recursive processes present in educational environments."[12] To be successful at this scale, the culture of the institution needs to encourage and promote the growth mindset in each interaction with students, but without mentioning it explicitly or teaching it as some kind of discrete programme. Students should encounter these encouragements repeatedly in many diverse aspects of their experience. In other words, small nudges over time – the flapping of a butterfly's wings – rather than an all-out sledgehammer assault on student attitudes and behaviours are more likely to yield benefits in terms of sustainable change.

I've got a growth mindset – where's my Nobel Prize?

A complicating factor with our "famous failures" and "growth mindset inspiration" posters was the tendency to use the exceptional as exemplars. The same is true of many of the personal stories used by Dweck, Duckworth, Gladwell, Syed, and others in their books. For understandable reasons, they focus on the outliers, the champions, the runaway successes in sport, business, education, music, technology, and art. This leads to the understandable confusion that somehow a growth mindset is going to unleash truly exceptional untapped potential in individuals if they just believe they can improve. Sadly, as we have already discussed, genetic predispositions and heritability *do* play a part in determining our potential; no matter how hard I train, I am never going to run faster that Usain Bolt. We can't all be outstanding; if we were, none of us would stand out.

There are many examples of fixed mindset successes – incredible talents who achieve great things on the strength of natural ability and circumstance alone. There are also millions of people who have a growth mindset and are moderately successful. Having a growth mindset does not make you exceptional. As Malcolm Gladwell shows, outliers are created by a combination of circumstance, system, and approach.[13] The only thing that a growth mindset, grit, and self-control will give you is a means to ensure you develop the talents that you have and continue to improve. If I don't believe that I can improve – if I believe that my running ability is fixed – then I won't work at it and I definitely won't get any better. But if I believe that I can improve, then I will train, and work, and then I will be able to run faster and further. Similarly, if I believe that I am "no good at maths" and, as a result of applying insufficient efforts, never experience success, than I am unlikely to invest time and effort into it, and consequently I am unlikely to improve – a vicious cycle. However, if I see that my efforts lead to achievements, however small to start with, then the application of that effort will be encouraged and a virtuous cycle can begin.

As Yeager and Walton point out, these approaches are "not magic." They are not suddenly going to make every student into a world-beater. But I firmly believe they offer the best route to continuous improvement, fulfilment, and development that we have in terms of school culture and climate.

The false growth mindset

As Dweck acknowledges in "We're still building the house," misunderstanding and misappropriation of her research ideas became rife as those ideas grew in popularity. Chief amongst her own concerns in this area is the "false growth mindset," which she explains in an interview with Christine Gross-Loh for *The Atlantic* in December 2016 (and elsewhere). Simply put, a false growth mindset is claiming to have a growth mindset when you don't actually have one, because you're aware of the theories and you know that it's better to say you have one than to admit to fixed mindset thinking. The irony of this is of course palpable. However, as Dweck explains,

> nobody has a growth mindset in everything all the time. Everyone is a mixture of fixed and growth mindsets. You could have a predominant growth mindset in an area but there can still be things that trigger you into a fixed mindset trait.[14]

We saw this in Angela Duckworth's instinctive reaction to student underperformance in Chapter 9.

One of the unfortunate side effects of this false growth mindset is the tendency to use praise for effort as a kind of consolation prize for failure: "oh, at least you tried hard." This is the misappropriation of her research that Dweck is most exercised about:

> The thing that keeps me up at night is that some educators are turning mindset into the new self-esteem, which is to make kids feel good about any effort they put in, whether they learn or not. But for me the growth mindset is a tool for learning and improvement. It's not just a vehicle for making children feel good.[15]

If children are praised for their effort when it is not linked to achievement, then they do not make the link between the two things. Trying hard becomes the end in itself, and this can be a fruitless endeavour if it does not lead to success, progress, and improvement. If students do not have effective learning strategies and techniques, then no amount of effort is going to help them to achieve. It will, instead, be a disheartening and frustrating experience. The classic examples of this are in the golf swing or the tennis serve: if technique is poor to start with and the player is not taught or coached effectively, practice will not lead to improvements in the serve or the swing. At worst, it will ingrain bad habits which can take much longer to unlearn and unpick. According to Dweck,

> students need to know that if they're stuck, they don't need just effort. You don't want them redoubling their efforts with the same ineffective strategies. You want them to know when to ask for help and when to use resources that are available.[16]

She continues on the same theme:

> A lot of parents or teachers say praise the effort, not the outcome. I say [that's] wrong: Praise the effort that led to the outcome or learning progress; tie the praise to it. It's not just effort, but strategy . . . so support the student in finding another strategy. Effective teachers who actually have classrooms full of children with a growth mindset are always supporting children's learning strategies and showing how strategies created that success.[17]

Failure should feel bad. It should be painful. We should all be motivated to work harder because we want to be successful. We should learn the lessons of failure so we can avoid those mistakes in the future, but also remember that success is the reward of applying purposeful effort. As Daniel Muijs and David Reynolds note, "the effect of achievement on self-concept is stronger than the effect of self-concept on achievement."[18] This is the way to build self-esteem with a growth mindset – teach children to value learning over the appearance of intelligence or cleverness, and to see challenge and struggle as necessary difficulties en route to eventual success.

Learning the lessons of failure

One of the most important lessons that I have learned in implementing a growth mindset ethos in schools is that you have to have a growth mindset about implementing a growth mindset ethos. Inevitably, changing and adapting a school culture is hard. The research and science supporting the approach is developing and evolving all the time. Some of the things we tried worked really well; others did not work as well as we had hoped. With hindsight, perhaps we could have predicted some of those missteps, but in any case we have continued to refine our understanding and have improved as a result. With our best growth mindset lenses in, we can say that we haven't cracked it . . . yet. But what we do know from our implementations so far is what works well, what is less effective, and what actively worked against us in schools.

Most effective

- Small, stealthy interventions

- Adjusting language and interaction across the school

- Focusing praise on strategies which lead to success and progress

- Working with students to change the learning culture

- Challenging teachers' implicit theories of intellect

- Patience

Not particularly effective

- Posters and displays

- Inspirational quotations

- "Famous failures" and "exceptional successes"

Worked against us

- Overusing explicit "growth mindset" terminology (led to "growth mindset fatigue")

- Written learning reflections to build growth mindsets (too onerous and led to resistance)

- Nagging

- Impatience

It takes time to build a growth mindset culture, and it's difficult. But we embrace challenge, and we persist in the face of setbacks; as Dweck says, "we're still building the house."[19]

Notes

1 Li & Bates, *Does Mindset Affect Children's Ability, School Achievement, or Response to Challenge?*, page 2.
2 Wilkinson, Rienzo, & Rolfe, "Changing mindsets."
3 Ibid., page 4.
4 Cummings, "Some thoughts on education and political priorities," page 74.
5 Herrnstein & Murray, *The Bell Curve*.
6 Taken from an interview with Robert Plomin by Peter Wilby in *The Guardian*.
7 Robert Plomin interviewed by Mary Wakefield for *The Spectator*.
8 Burnette et al., "Mind-sets matter."
9 Dweck, "Growth mindset is on a firm foundation."
10 Ibid.
11 Yeager & Walton, "Social-psychological interventions in education."

12 Ibid., page 267.
13 Gladwell, *Outliers*.
14 Dweck quoted by Christine Gross-Loh in *The Atlantic*: "How praise became a consolation prize."
15 Dweck interviewed by John Dickens for *Schools Week*.
16 Gross-Loh, op. cit.
17 Ibid.
18 Muijs & Reynolds, *Effective Teaching*, page 147.
19 Dweck, op. cit.

Bibliography

Burnette, J.L., O'Boyle, E.H., VanEpps, E.M., Pollack, J.M., & Finkel, E.J. (2013, May). Mindsets matter: A meta-analytic review of implicit theories and self-regulation. *Psychological Bulletin*, *139*(3), 655–701.

Cummings, D. (2013). Some thoughts on education and political priorities. Retrieved 17 April, 2017, from: http://s3.documentcloud.org/documents/804396/some-thoughts-on-education-and-political.pdf

Department for Education. (2016, 12 April). Awards launched for schools best at instilling character. Retrieved 11 April, 2017, from *GOV.UK*: https://www.gov.uk/government/news/awards-launched-for-schools-best-at-instilling-character

Dickens, J. (2015, 18 June). Carol Dweck says mindset is not a tool to make children feel good. Retrieved 18 April, 2017, from *Schools Week*: http://schoolsweek.co.uk/why-mindset-is-not-a-tool-to-make-children-feel-good/

Dweck, C. (2017, 18 January). Growth mindset is on a firm foundation, but we're still building the house. Retrieved 17 April, 2017, from *Mindset Scholars Network*: http://mindsetscholarsnetwork.org/growth-mindset-firm-foundation-still-building-house/

Gladwell, M. (2009). *Outliers*. London: Penguin.

Gross-Loh, C. (2016, 16 December). How praise became a consolation prize. Retrieved 31 December, 2016, from *The Atlantic*: https://www.theatlantic.com/education/archive/2016/12/how-praise-became-a-consolation-prize/510845/

Herrnstein, R.J., & Murray, C. (1994). *The Bell Curve: Intelligence and Class Structure in American Life*. New York: Free Press.

Li, Y., & Bates, T.C. (2017, 23 January). Does growth mindset improve children's IQ, educational attainment or response to setbacks? Active-control interventions and data on children's own mindsets. Retrieved 17 April, 2017, from *SocArXiv*: https://osf.io/preprints/socarxiv/tsdwy

Muijs, D., & Reynolds, D. (2011). *Effective Teaching: Evidence and Practice*. London: Sage Publications.

Wakefield, M. (2013, 27 July). Revealed: How exam results owe more to genes than teaching. Retrieved 17 April, 2017, from *The Spectator*: https://www.spectator.co.uk/2013/07/sorry-but-intelligence-really-is-in-the-genes/

Wilby, P. (2014, 18 February). Psychologist on a mission to give every child a Learning Chip. Retrieved 17 April, 2017, from *The Guardian*: https://www.theguardian.com/education/2014/feb/18/psychologist-robert-plomin-says-genes-crucial-education

Wilkinson, D., Rienzo, C., & Rolfe, H. (2015, June). Changing mindsets. Retrieved 17 April, 2017, from *Education Endowment Foundation*: https://v1.educationendowmentfoundation.org.uk/uploads/pdf/Changing_Mindsets.pdf

Yeager, D.S., & Walton, G.M. (2011, 1 June). Social-psychological interventions in education: They're not magic. *Review of Educational Research*, *81*(2), 267–301.

Towards a growth mindset culture

Over the course of this book I hope I have shown that "having a growth mindset" is not a simple or binary choice. There is a continuum between fixed and growth mindsets for all of us, and our mindsets are domain-specific – nobody has a completely fixed or a completely growth mindset, and we are likely to have more of a fixed mindset or more of a growth mindset in particular aspects of our life and learning than in others. I also hope I have shown that having a growth mindset is not enough, in isolation, to provide the magic solution to academic achievement and progress. We need a rich and challenging curriculum within which to apply our mindset, with expert teachers guiding and instructing our learning through carefully targeted feedback. We need the security of a safe and orderly school environment to allow us to expose ourselves to the risks of taking on new challenges. And we need internally embedded self-control mechanisms so that we can apply ourselves purposefully to the task in hand, free from superfluous or irrelevant distractions.

Whilst growth mindset is not a panacea, there is a substantial body of evidence that a whole range of "non-cognitive"[1] qualities have a significant impact on student achievement and well-being. As enthusiasm for grit and growth mindset has grown, there has been an associated lack of clarity over what exactly those non-cognitive qualities are. Angela Duckworth and David Yeager include "goal-directed effort (e.g., grit, self-control, growth mindset), healthy social relationships (e.g., gratitude, emotional intelligence, social belonging), and sound judgment and decision making (e.g., curiosity, open-mindedness)"[2] in their assessment of the various qualities. All of these are difficult to measure, and using any such measures in any kind of accountability framework is riven with problems. But each of them has been shown to be a powerful predictor of academic, economic, social, psychological, and physical well-being. It is no wonder that teachers, schools, and educators the world over are working hard to develop those qualities in the young people they teach.

Carol Dweck, alongside colleagues Gregory Walton and Geoffrey Cohen, describes the combination of those non-cognitive qualities as "academic tenacity."[3] Academically tenacious students:

- Belong academically and socially

- See school as relevant to their future

- Work hard and can postpone immediate pleasures

- Are not derailed by intellectual or social difficulties

- Seek out challenges

- Remain engaged over the long haul[4]

The best possible outcomes come from the meshing of growth mindset, grit, and Marshmallow Test self-control with an inclusive culture which ensures that each individual is valued by and sees the value in the school to which they belong. Although some students will already possess these qualities due to the culture of their family, community, and prior learning, all of them can be taught and all of them can be learned. However, there is no one-off lesson plan or resource pack that is going to build a culture of academic tenacity. A growth mindset culture is built on more than an inspirational assembly and a series of motivational posters. To build grit, self-control, growth mindset, social belonging, curiosity, gratitude, and emotional intelligence, the culture of the school needs to value and reflect these qualities. They need to be woven into the fabric of the institution such that every system is aligned and every interaction directs staff and students towards the development of these qualities. In its simplest form, a growth mindset needs to be "how we do things here."

Challenge and scaffolding

For students – for any learners – to develop academic tenacity, they need to experience challenge not just occasionally but consistently throughout their education. Each learning experience, in lessons and in the extra-curricular programme, needs to be designed to reinforce the connection between effort and achievement. To me, this is what "high expectations" means: students need to come to school expecting to have to work hard. If they grasp things quickly or easily, then teaching needs to be designed to ramp up the challenge until they are struggling, then hold them at that level of difficulty as they make progress. That progress should be tangible – students should be able to look back and see how far they've come, recognising that the effort they have put in has got them there. Struggle should be valued and celebrated as a result.

High expectations should not, however, result in unattainable goals. It is vital for all of us to know where it is that we are heading with a particular task, unit, or module, and to know that the end goal is achievable at some level. With diligent effort and continuous reinforcement of the progress being made, we can all be encouraged to push ourselves one step further onwards. But when students struggle, a growth mindset response must be to resist the temptation of differentiating the expectation downwards – or worse, doing the task for them – and, instead, see what support is needed to enable the students to meet the expectation. More time? A different technique? A recap? An additional or alternative resource? With the scaffolding in place, we must support our students to reach the full height of the cathedral, but also be sure that the structure will remain standing once the scaffolding has been taken away.

Central to the reinforcement of high expectations in this way is the challenge to teachers' own implicit theories of intellect. Do the teachers genuinely believe that all students can reach the high expectations that we have for them? If they don't believe it, the students will know. No matter how well we try and disguise it, if we are thinking that "there's no way he'll get this" or that "she'll never be able to achieve that," they will know. We have to believe that all students can achieve, in order to help them believe it about themselves.

Belonging: what is your why?

We need to be clear about the purpose of our shared endeavour in schools. Why is it that we are educating our young people in the first place? Is it so they can get a good grade in their GCSEs? So that the school's Progress 8 score remains high and avoids attention from the inspectorate? Or because we have to? These are all extrinsic motivators, powerful in their own way but ultimately unfulfilling. It is worth asking the question of yourself, and of your colleagues – why are we doing this? Each individual will have their own story, their own "why."[5] At Churchill, when we considered this question, we came up with the statement "to inspire and enable young people to make a positive difference."[6] Our purpose in educating our young people is to provide them with the ability to make the world a better place. If we do our job properly and turn out well-balanced, lifelong learners with all of the academic tenacity that a growth mindset brings, they will improve society and the world we live in as a result.

Articulating our "why" and applying it consistently on a whole-school level helps all of us to focus on the intrinsic motivation of the learning process – that a good education improves not only us as individuals but the world around us as well. David Yeager and others have found that articulating a "self-transcendent purpose for learning" can foster self-regulation,[7] improving the academic tenacity described by Dweck and raising grades in Maths and Science, especially for lower-attaining students. This finding tallies with the argument that having a sense of purpose is a stronger intrinsic motivator than any external enticement of grades or physical rewards. As Daniel Pink defines it, a "purpose" is "the yearning to do what we do in the service of something larger than ourselves."[8] When we "start with why"[9] rather than "what" we do, we bind ourselves together into a shared endeavour which begins to shape the sense of belonging that underpins the success of any communal enterprise.

If we are to be successful in our mission to become a growth mindset school – to set no limits on what we can achieve – then each and every interaction needs to be focused on that shared purpose. That comes down to being genuinely interested in each individual not because of the grades they might achieve but because of the difference they could make to themselves, to their family, to the school community, and to wider society if their energy and ability were harnessed and directed.

Building a growth mindset culture

Each school's culture and ethos is unique, influenced by its context, location, history, traditions, and community. It seems obvious, therefore, that any one-size-fits-all solution to building culture and ethos in a school is doomed to failure. Yet the idea of a growth mindset is not one-size-fits-all. It is a concept that can transcend the differences between individual contexts and cultures and be applied effectively in one family, one teacher's classroom, a small village primary school, or a large urban secondary. Instilling the belief that hard work and carefully applied effort will lead to improvements in ability is something that all schools can subscribe to, whether your school is founded on the principles of faith, on the basis of modern technology, or on resolutely traditional teaching methods. In the classrooms I have taught in and the schools I have led, I have attempted to build this culture so that the habits of academic tenacity will benefit the students not only whilst they are under my care, but beyond into the rest of their lives. I know that there is still much to discover and much to do, and I know the work is not finished.

Yet.

Notes

1 Duckworth & Yeager, "Measurement Matters."
2 Ibid., page 237.
3 Dweck, Walton, & Cohen, *Academic Tenacity*.
4 Ibid., page 4.
5 Simon Sinek writes persuasively about why we should "start with why."
6 The full vision and values statement can be seen on the school website: www.churchill-academy.org/Information/Vision-Ethos/
7 Yeager et al.'s study, "Boring but important: A self-transcendent purpose for learning fosters academic self-regulation" is cited by Angela Duckworth in *Grit*, page 166.
8 Pink, *Drive*, page 204.
9 Sinek, op. cit.

Bibliography

Baldwin, J. (1991). *Nobody Knows My Name: More Notes of a Native Son*. London: Penguin Classics.

Churchill Academy & Sixth Form. (2017, 19 July). Vision and values. Retrieved 27 July, 2017, from *Churchill Academy & Sixth Form*: www.churchill-academy.org/Information/Vision-Ethos/

Duckworth, A. (2016). *Grit*. London: Vermilion.

Duckworth, A. L., & Yeager, D. S. (2015). Measurement matters: Assessing personal qualities other than cognitive ability for educational purposes. *Educational Researcher, 44*(4), 237–251.

Dweck, C. S., Walton, G. M., & Cohen, G. L. (2014). *Academic Tenacity: Mindsets and Skills that Promote Long-Term Learning*. Seattle, WA: Bill & Melinda Gates Foundation.

Mclean, A. (2003). *The Motivated School*. London: Sage Publications Ltd.

Pink, D. (2011). *Drive*. Edinburgh: Canongate Books.

Sinek, S. (2011). *Start with Why*. London: Penguin.

Yeager, D. S., Henderson, M. D., Paunesku, D., Walton, G. M., D'Mello, S., Spitzer, B. J., & Duckworth, A. (2014). Boring but important: A self-transcendent purpose for learning fosters academic self-regulation. *Journal of Personality and Social Psychology, 107*(4), 559–580.

Index